NARROWING THE DISASTER RISK PROTECTION GAP IN CENTRAL ASIA

SEPTEMBER 2022

© 2022 Asian Development Bank
6 ADB Avenue, Mandaluyong City, 1550 Metro Manila, Philippines
Tel +63 2 8632 4444; Fax +63 2 8636 2444
www.adb.org

Some rights reserved. Published in 2022.

ISBN 978-92-9269-679-5 (print); 978-92-9269-680-1 (electronic); 978-92-9269-681-8 (ebook)
Publication Stock No. TCS220333-2
DOI: http://dx.doi.org/10.22617/TCS220333-2

Notes:
In this publication, "$" refers to United States dollars.
ADB recognizes "China" as the People's Republic of China, and "Kyrgyzstan" as the Kyrgyz Republic.

Cover design by Francis Manio.

On the cover: All CAREC member countries have a deficit of robust risk financing. With common risks faced from floods and earthquakes, regional solutions can help narrow the protection gap and provide quick and reliable access to finance to support immediate response and recovery efforts.

Contents

Tables, Figures, and Box

Tables

Figures

Box

Acknowledgments

This study was undertaken on behalf of the Central Asia Regional Economic Cooperation (CAREC) Secretariat and the Asian Development Bank (ADB) under the technical assistance, *Developing a Disaster Risk Transfer Facility in the CAREC Region*. The team would like to thank Junkyu Lee, director, Chief Financial Sector Group, Sustainable Development and Climate Change Department (SDCC); Lyaziza Sabyrova, director, Regional Cooperation and Operations Coordination Division, Central and West Asia Department (CWRD); Safdar Parvez, advisor, Office of the Director General, East Asia Department; Thomas Kessler, principal finance specialist (Disaster Insurance), SDCC; Carmen Garcia Perez, regional cooperation specialist, CWRD; Irene de Roma, programs officer, CWRD; Jennifer Lapis, CAREC regional cooperation coordinator; and Alzeus Alzate, CAREC administrative assistant, for the overall support and guidance.

The team also expresses its appreciation to the regional cooperation coordinators and national focal points' advisors in all CAREC countries for their assistance in organizing and hosting virtual consultations. The team would also like to extend its gratitude to senior officials in CAREC countries for their inputs, feedback, and contributions.

The authors of this study were John Ward at Pengwern Associates with research support from Joe Peissel and Pieter Sayer; and Christopher Au, David Simmons, and Stuart Calam at Willis Towers Watson. Data contributions have been provided by the Global Earthquake Model Foundation and JBA Risk Management.

Abbreviations

AAL	average annual loss
ADB	Asian Development Bank
AZN	Azerbaijani manat
BISP	Benazir Income Support Programme
CAREC	Central Asia Regional Economic Cooperation
CCRIF	Caribbean Catastrophe Risk Insurance Facility
COVID-19	coronavirus disease
DMC	developing member country
GDP	gross domestic product
GEL	Georgian lari
GNI	gross national income
HDI	Human Development Index
IBLI	Index Based Livestock Insurance
IMF	International Monetary Fund
JICA	Japan International Cooperation Agency
LGFV	Local Government Financing Vehicle
PRs	Pakistani rupees
PRC	People's Republic of China
SMEs	small and medium-sized enterprises
SRSP	Shock Responsive Social Protection
TA	technical assistance
UN	United Nations
UNICEF	United Nations Children's Fund

Executive Summary

This report discusses and estimates the "protection gap" for flood and earthquake disaster risk in the Central Asia Regional Economic Cooperation (CAREC) region. The intention of the study is to better understand the current approach to disaster risk finance in each member country, to identify opportunities to strengthen financing arrangements. The report also inputs into the design of the regional disaster risk transfer facility to be developed under this technical assistance.

When flood and earthquake disaster events happen, finance is required by those experiencing the consequences of that risk—the "risk holder." This finance is needed first to support immediate response and recovery efforts before longer term reconstruction. Quick and reliable access to such finance, for both sovereign and subsovereign governments, as well as households and businesses, is critical in minimizing the human losses that disaster events cause.

Some of this financing can be arranged in advance of a disaster. These so-called ex ante mechanisms have the advantage that many of the decisions regarding their structure and use—such as how much will be provided, to which parties, and for which activities—are already determined. This typically means that ex ante mechanisms can provide finance more quickly, and the amount of finance they provide is more predictable, than if financing arrangements are only made after the disaster strikes (ex post). Ex ante mechanisms can be further distinguished between risk retention mechanisms, where the financial resources are provided by the risk holder (e.g., reserve funds, savings, contingent disaster financing), and risk-transfer mechanisms where the responsibility for providing financial resources in the event of a disaster is transferred to a third party (e.g., insurance).

The quantification of the protection gap in this report is based on the difference between the losses from disaster events and the extent of available ex ante finance. This focus on ex ante mechanisms reflects the predictability and timeliness that these financing sources provide, which evidence shows is critical in reducing the impact of disasters. In undertaking these calculations, the report considers different types of losses that might need to be covered by ex ante mechanisms including emergency response costs, the losses associated with the reconstruction of property, as well as the indirect losses that disaster events might pose in terms of, for example, business interruption. It also considers the finance that might be required on average each year, as well as the finance that might be required when events of different frequency and severity strike.

While ex ante mechanisms are crucial, governments, households, and businesses may also access finance through ex post mechanisms, most notably through assuming additional debt. However, the feasibility and desirability of using ex post mechanisms varies substantially. In countries with robust macroeconomic fundamentals, easy access to credit and where business and households benefit from high levels of financial inclusion, ex post borrowing may relatively be easy. Generous social protection measures will also reduce the borrowing households require and/or make it easier for them to access such funds. By contrast, where the opposite is true, ex post borrowing is unlikely to be feasible or desirable. In these cases, both governments and individuals may end up relying, instead, on humanitarian support. While such support plays a vital role, its amount, speed, and predictability rarely match the needs of the beneficiaries. As such, to complement the quantitative assessment of the protection gap, the report also provides a qualitative discussion on the feasibility of both governments and households relying on ex post borrowing or other non-humanitarian response measures to cope with disasters. This analysis allows some broad categories of CAREC member countries to be distinguished.

The first group are those countries with the largest protection gap consisting of Afghanistan, Pakistan, and Tajikistan. In these countries, ex ante risk finance measures are limited, such that more than 85% of the average annual losses (AAL) are not covered. The paucity of financing means even frequent events are likely to exhaust any risk retention mechanisms. The challenges in these countries are compounded by low sovereign credit ratings, which will make it difficult and more expensive to access debt from private capital markets, and low rates of financial inclusion of households, which affects the financial resilience of citizens. Moreover, in all three countries, the provinces where risk and vulnerability coincide most strongly are characterized by a heavy reliance on agriculture and basic agro-processing, largely undertaken by smallholder farmers and small and medium-sized enterprises. In Tajikistan and Pakistan, the greatest financing needs relate to flood events. In Afghanistan, earthquakes are a greater challenge. There is an urgent need to enhance all aspects of disaster risk financing: at the sovereign and the household levels; for common events (where risk retention is often more appropriate) and rarer events (where risk transfer is often more appropriate). The ability to pay for additional disaster risk finance will, however, be a critical challenge, although this should be seen in the context of the even higher costs that can be expected from disaster events if there is no ex ante financing in place.

A second group consists of the Kyrgyz Republic, Uzbekistan, and Mongolia. These countries all benefit from some risk retention mechanisms and have somewhat greater financial resilience to the most common disaster events than countries in the first group. Both the sovereign governments and households are also somewhat more likely to access borrowing than countries in the first group. The context across these three countries also differs in important ways. The Kyrgyz Republic is expected to see the largest losses of any country in the CAREC region as a percentage of gross national income, due to both extensive flood and earthquake risk. It is estimated that just over 50% of its AAL are not covered by risk retention or risk transfer mechanisms. Recent economic development in Uzbekistan provides stronger macroeconomic fundamentals, though risk varies spatially, revealing large areas of acute vulnerability. It is estimated that just under 85% of its AAL are not covered by risk transfer or risk reduction mechanisms. In Mongolia, the overall level of risk is lower than other CAREC countries, reducing the relative size of the financing need. Indeed, in contrast to the other two countries in this category, the central case results suggest that there could be sufficient ex ante risk finance in place to cover the AAL associated with floods and earthquakes (although in previous disaster events not all the budgeted funding has been made available). In addition, well-targeted social protection measures and moderate financial inclusion and insurance penetration mean there is a broader base of resilience across the country than in other countries in the region. However, the strained fiscal position of the government means that it is unlikely to quickly and easily rely on ex post borrowing to meet the funding needs associated with disasters. In the Kyrgyz Republic and Uzbekistan, risk and vulnerability overlap most acutely in areas where agricultural and manufacturing activities are both important. In Mongolia, livestock herding is the most important economic activity in the locations of greatest concern.

A third group of countries consists of Azerbaijan, Georgia, and Kazakhstan. All these countries have reasonably good access to finance to help respond to disaster events. Existing risk retention mechanisms are sufficient to cover AAL from flood and earthquake events and/or cover the emergency response costs of more severe events (typically up to 1 in 200-year events). A further common feature of these countries is that the provinces where risk and vulnerability coincide rely less heavily on agriculture than similar regions in the other groupings with, instead, activities such as light manufacturing, and, in the case of Kazakhstan, fossil fuel extraction and refining, dominating the economic structures of the relevant regions. However, at present, the direct losses of 1 in 10-year flood event in Kazakhstan or a 1 in 5-year flood event in Georgia would exhaust current risk retention mechanisms, rising, respectively, to a 1 in 100-year and 1 in 25-year earthquake event. As such, in these countries, the greatest need may be for risk transfer instruments that would support reconstruction for events of these thresholds of severity or greater.

A final group consists of Turkmenistan and Inner Mongolia Autonomous Region and Xinjiang Uygur Autonomous Region in the People's Republic of China. It is more difficult to draw definitive conclusions regarding the protection gap for these CAREC member countries and provinces. Data availability is an issue for Turkmenistan. In the case of Xinjiang Uygur Autonomous Region and Inner Mongolia Autonomous Region, government support for disaster events is centralized. This means that an understanding of the extent to which current funding mechanisms are adequate for these provinces would require an assessment of the risks throughout the country as only then would it be possible to understand whether the amount of funding available to each province would be sufficient. This has not been conducted.

All CAREC member countries have a deficit of robust risk financing for flood and earthquake disaster risk. The varying levels of financing are testament to the progress made by some governments over several years. Others, meanwhile, face a high level of disaster risk without sufficient financial protection. Even where governments have arranged financing, the modest quantum means these are likely to be exhausted rapidly. Rates of economic development are increasing the value-at-risk over time. An intensification of rainfall patterns consistent with climate change predictions increases the potency of the hazard. Without a committed response, the protection gap is likely to widen further.

A regional approach to disaster risk management and financing could benefit many countries simultaneously. With common risks faced from floods and earthquakes, regional cooperation solutions can materially narrow the protection gap. A regional facility, as targeted under this technical assistance, can provide an optimally and sustainably priced insurance capacity for countries and so increase the amount of ex ante financing for disasters. For example, with current emergency response financing requirements exhausted for many CAREC countries between 1 in 5-year and 1 in 20-year events, a regional solution could provide insurance cover at these levels for the respective member countries. This would quickly offer a financing solution for CAREC member countries, and materially narrow the protection gap for disaster risk.

Introduction

The Central Asia Regional Economic Cooperation (CAREC) region is highly exposed to disaster events.[1] Geophysical, atmospheric, and hydrometeorological disaster events inflict losses on a frequent basis. The modeling analysis undertaken for this project suggests that floods and earthquakes cause average annual loss (AAL)[2] of $4.7 billion across the region. Recent economic development of CAREC member countries has increased the value at risk (e.g., asset growth in quality and quantity). Governments increasingly seek financial protection against the asset losses associated with disaster events. The extent of this financing varies between countries and invariably lags that of total disaster risk.

This report provides an assessment and quantification of the protection gap across all CAREC member countries. The protection gap is traditionally defined as the proportion of losses from disaster events that are not insured. Identifying the level of risk that has not been reduced (through risk reduction investment) or transferred (through risk financing) involves identifying the contingent liability that needs to be met in the event of a disaster. This is used as a fundamental input into the design of risk management and arrangement of risk financing.

This study is part of the Asian Development Bank (ADB) technical assistance (TA) to CAREC member countries to strengthen their disaster risk management strategies and public sector budget resilience. It builds on the disaster risk profiling work conducted by using these modeled loss figures as the basis for quantifying the disaster risk for each member country. It then assesses the extent to which financing is available to meet these losses, and hence the size of the protection gap. It is intended to provide guidance on how a regional disaster risk transfer facility (to be developed under this TA) may meet the needs of governments and citizens.

This report aims to take a comprehensive approach to assessing the protection gap. It considers not just the extent to which the losses associated with disaster events may be insured (i.e., the extent to which risk transfer mechanisms are in place to meet the contingent liabilities of disasters), but also the extent to which governments may have set up well-functioning risk retention mechanisms to help meet some of these losses. It also considers both ex ante and ex post mechanisms, recognizing that governments and households can use additional debt to finance risk.

This comprehensive approach to assessing and quantifying the protection gap is consistent with risk-layering principles. Such principles recognize that insurance risk transfer solutions are only one element of a strategy for financing the contingent liabilities associated with disasters and that a portfolio of strategies differing according to the frequency and severity of events, could and should be used.

---

[1] CAREC member countries are Afghanistan, Azerbaijan, Georgia, Kazakhstan, the Kyrgyz Republic, Mongolia, Pakistan, the People's Republic of China (Inner Mongolia Autonomous Region [IMAR], and Xinjiang Uygur Autonomous Region [XUAR]), Tajikistan, Turkmenistan, and Uzbekistan. ADB placed on hold its assistance to Afghanistan effective 15 August 2021. All references to Afghanistan in this report are based on information available as of 30 July 2021.

[2] AAL refers to the long-term expected losses per year from disaster events, averaging out low severity events that happen relatively frequently with more severe events that only occur infrequently.

The report provides an assessment of the economic losses that flood and earthquake risk might pose to each country. It details how these risks are distributed across the country and how these overlap with areas of poverty. This allows identification of areas where both risks and vulnerability are high. It then analyzes the extent to which a combination of insurance and ex ante risk retention mechanisms (such as reserve funds, lines of contingent credit, etc.) are already available to governments, households, and businesses. This provides an assessment of the potentially unfunded liabilities that the country may face, including the severity and frequency of an event that could exhaust existing risk retention and risk transfer arrangements. Finally, the macroeconomic context and the extent of financial inclusion and comprehensiveness of social protection mechanisms are considered to understand whether it may be feasible for governments, households, and businesses to rely on ex post borrowing, or otherwise access financial resources to meet the losses associated with flood and earthquake events in the country. Together, this provides a combined quantitative–qualitative assessment of the protection gap.

Disaster Risk Finance and Methodological Approach

Principles of Disaster Risk Finance

A key priority for all those who face disaster risk—governments, businesses, and households—is to seek to effectively reduce the severity of the risks that they face. This risk reduction might include physical interventions such as building flood defenses and retrofitting property, but also planning activities such as risk-based site selection for new developments, and evacuation and response plans.[3]

However, even if risk reduction is well-planned and executed, residual risk is likely to remain. As such, when disaster events strike, it is essential that governments, businesses, and households have timely access to sufficient and reliable financial resources to recover the losses associated with these residual risks. These resources help with the initial response (e.g., debris removal or emergency shelter and health care) as well as to facilitate reconstruction of assets in the longer term. An underlying objective is to return the economy to a functioning response as fast as possible, and to reduce the negative impact of the event. The longer reconstruction and recovery take, the greater the economic losses.

The need for these financial resources is a contingent liability that the risk holders will be expected to meet. When combined with well-articulated plans as to how these resources will be used, adequate and reliable financing of these contingent liabilities can critically speed up response and reconstruction efforts, substantially reducing human loss and suffering that would otherwise materialize. A range of different sources of finance are available. Figure 1 shows one way of categorizing these different sources.

An important distinction between ex ante and ex post sources of finance needs to be made. Ex ante mechanisms are arranged before an event occurs. This allows decisions on who will be responsible for providing how much finance, and the terms on which that finance will be provided, to be taken without the pressures and strains associated with responding to a disaster event. They can be contrasted with ex post mechanisms where decisions and actions on accessing the finance are only taken after an event happens. This might include unplanned borrowing, budget reallocation or making use of humanitarian support.

As Figure 1 shows, within the group of ex ante mechanisms, a further distinction can be made between risk retention and risk transfer. Risk retention mechanisms are financial resources that are provided[4] by the risk holder and include reserve funds, contingent disaster financing, etc. These can be contrasted with risk transfer mechanisms where, in exchange for a premium, the responsibility for providing financial resources in a disaster event is transferred to a third party. As such, risk transfer instruments redistribute the infrequent and potentially unmanageable total losses of a disaster event into an equivalent manageable annual cost (premium). Risk transfer instruments include a range of different insurance products as well as alternative risk transfer instruments such as catastrophe or disaster relief bonds.

---

[3] C. Meenan, J. Ward and R. Muir-Wood. 2019. *Disaster Risk Finance - A Toolkit*. Deutsche Gesellschaft für Internationale Zusammenarbeit (GIZ) GmbH. https://www.indexinsuranceforum.org/sites/default/files/Publikationen03_DRF_ACRI_DINA4_WEB_190617.pdf.

[4] Or for which the liability is assumed by the risk holder.

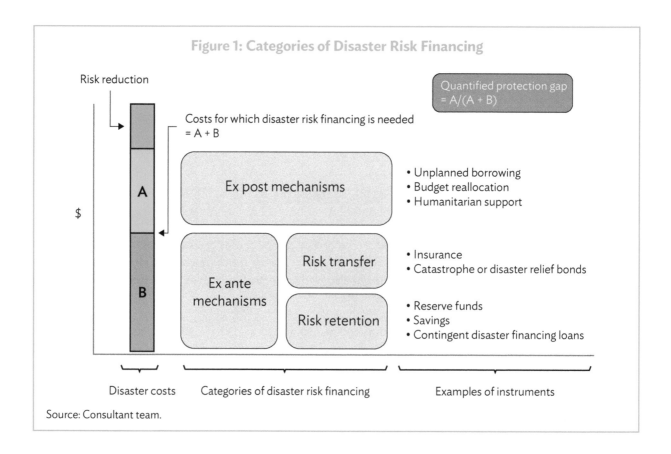

Figure 1: Categories of Disaster Risk Financing

Risk reduction

Quantified protection gap
= A/(A + B)

Costs for which disaster risk financing is needed
= A + B

$

A — Ex post mechanisms
- Unplanned borrowing
- Budget reallocation
- Humanitarian support

B — Ex ante mechanisms

Risk transfer
- Insurance
- Catastrophe or disaster relief bonds

Risk retention
- Reserve funds
- Savings
- Contingent disaster financing loans

Disaster costs   Categories of disaster risk financing   Examples of instruments

Source: Consultant team.

A disaster risk finance strategy sets out how the contingent liabilities created by disaster events will be financed through a combination of ex ante and ex post mechanisms, and the balance between and within these different categories. Four key principles can help guide the creation of such strategies:

(i)   **A strong focus on ex ante instruments can speed up access to financial resources following a disaster event, hence reducing the suffering and losses that it otherwise causes.**[5] By removing the need to determine or negotiate the terms on which resources can be accessed, and reducing the uncertainty regarding how much resources might be available, ex ante instruments allow both governments and households to access resources more quickly and program their use more efficiently than might otherwise be the case. Furthermore, as credit rating agencies have identified, in the context of analysis into the physical risks of climate change, frequent disaster events can themselves may make it more difficult for governments to borrow easily and cheaply.[6] These factors explain why this report focuses on the extent to which ex ante funding mechanisms are in place and quantifies the protection gap in terms of the extent to which these arrangements are not in place and instead require a country to rely on ex post mechanisms. At the same time, ex post mechanisms provide flexibility to deal with unexpected consequences of disasters and do not require financial commitments to be made ahead of the disaster events, allowing funds instead to be spent elsewhere. This may be particularly attractive to governments, households, and businesses who, because of their financial robustness, are confident that even after a disaster event strikes, they can nonetheless access ex post finance quickly and cheaply. Assessing this opportunity cost is important to determine the mix of arrangements in a disaster risk financing strategy.

---

[5]   D. Clarke and S. Dercon. 2016. *Dull Disasters?: How Planning Ahead Will Make a Difference.* New York: Oxford University Press.
[6]   Moody's Investor Service. 2021. *Physical climate risk is credit negative for most sovereigns, particularly in emerging markets.* 6 May. https://www. moodys.com/research/Moodys-Physical-climate-risk-is-credit-negative-for-most-sovereigns--PBC_1282314?cid=7QFRKQSZE021.

(ii)   **Instruments should be matched for the different types of costs and losses following a disaster event.** Immediately after an event, there are a range of operational and humanitarian response costs (e.g., medical assistance). Ensuring quick access to financial resources can dramatically reduce the social and economic impact. This is then followed by a longer term, typically larger, but less urgent, need for funding to support reconstruction. For this activity, confidence that the financial resources will be sufficient to meet the associated losses is of great importance.

(iii) **Events of differing frequency and severity are likely to demand different types of financial instruments.** Broadly speaking, risk retention instruments are better suited for meeting the losses associated with high frequency and relatively low intensity events. This is because the costs of risk retention are not going to be so high as to substantially reduce spending on other priorities that a government, household, or business might have. Equally, the frequency of such events may make the premiums associated with risk transfer instruments unattractive. By contrast, it is likely to be very costly to retain the risks associated with low-frequency, high-severity events, and so risk transfer may be more appropriate. For the most extreme events, insurance may not be available, and it may be necessary to rely on donor assistance. Figure 2 illustrates this principle of risk-layering as it applies to governments, although a broadly similar approach is also relevant for households and businesses.

(iv)   **Pooling arrangements can help reduce the costs of risk transfer.** Pooling refers to arrangements whereby different entities that could consider risk transfer arrangements independently decide instead to act collaboratively and organize and purchase risk transfer as a collective unit. This can help reduce the costs of risk transfer in two ways. First, because different entities within a pool have different risk profiles, acting collectively provides a diversification benefit as the volatility in the financing needs of the pool as a whole is lower than the volatility of each individual entity. This reduced volatility feeds through into a lower cost for transferring risk. Second, organizing and purchasing risk transfer products requires a series of unavoidable fixed costs such as licensing, structuring, set-up, administrative, and claims management costs. Acting collectively allows these costs to be shared, reducing the overall average cost of risk transfer.

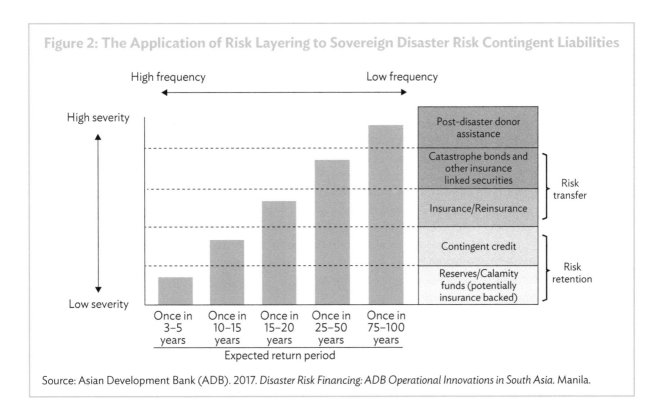

Figure 2: The Application of Risk Layering to Sovereign Disaster Risk Contingent Liabilities

Source: Asian Development Bank (ADB). 2017. *Disaster Risk Financing: ADB Operational Innovations in South Asia*. Manila.

Methodology

The purpose of this report is to compare the risks associated with earthquake and flood in each of the CAREC countries with the financing approaches used by governments, households, and businesses. This can help identify where and what type of additional disaster risk financing may be most valuable in each country and regionally. The report utilizes the same methodology for each CAREC country, to the extent the data allow, and the discussion is structured in the same way. Each country is assessed by

(i)   applying catastrophe risk modeling to understand the direct and indirect economic losses for each country,
(ii) reviewing existing ex ante risk financing arrangements,
(iii) comparing the gap between the modeled losses and ex ante arrangements,
(iv) considering other available sources of financing to close the gap, and
(v)   providing initial conclusions.

Box: Key Terms

- **Average annual loss.** The long-term expected losses per year from disaster events. It takes account both low severity events that happen relatively frequently with more severe events that only occur infrequently.
- **Direct loss.** The cost of replacing assets damaged or destroyed by disaster events. In this analysis, direct losses focus on the damage to residential, industrial, and commercial property.
- **Indirect loss.** The loss in income (output) that arises over the medium term because of the direct loss.
- **Return period.** The expected (average) time between events of the same severity. For example, it would be expected that the average length of time between two 1 in 10-year events would be 10 years.

Source: Consultant team.

The starting point is to identify the magnitude of the losses that flood and earthquake risk might cause. Referring to Figure 1, these are the losses for which disaster risk financing is needed. This draws upon modeling undertaken previously and primarily focuses on the direct losses (i.e., the replacement costs of the assets damaged or destroyed by different events). It should be stressed the estimates of direct losses are conservative estimates as they only focus on residential, industrial, and commercial property. This means, for example, that agricultural losses and the direct losses faced by infrastructure are excluded from the direct loss figure. The analysis does, however, consider the indirect losses that disaster events might cause. These relate to the ongoing reduction in income (output) that events might cause because, for example, businesses are unable to operate or because they suffer supply-chain disruptions, etc. Some of these reductions in income (output) are likely to require disaster risk financing as governments choose or are required to provide compensation for this reduction in income. The section also provides information on the expected human loss that disaster events may cause. Finally, it provides a brief sub-national analysis comparing estimates of expected economic and human loss with subnational data on poverty,[7]

---

[7]   Where data is available, the subnational estimates of poverty are taken from the Multidimensional Poverty Index from the Oxford Poverty and Human Development Initiative. https://ophi.org.uk/multidimensional-poverty-index/#:~:text=The%20global%20 Multidimensional%20Poverty%20Index,that%20a%20person%20faces%20simultaneously. This is the preferred data source as it complements monetary poverty measures by capturing deprivations in health, education, and living standards that a person faces simultaneously. The dataset also provides information on the number/proportion of people living in poverty. However, this dataset is not available for all CAREC countries so, where necessary, data on the human development index score at the subnational level was used instead (https://globaldatalab.org/shdi/shdi/). The human development index aggregates information on life expectancy, education, and per capita income, and converts this to an index score of between 0 and 1 with scores closer to 1 representing higher levels of human development.

recognizing that poverty is likely to accentuate the vulnerability of the population to disaster events in ways that are not fully captured by catastrophe modeling. This allows the initial identification of subnational "hot spots" where both hazard risk is high and poverty, relative to elsewhere in the country, is also high. The key economic activities undertaken, especially those conducted by small and medium-sized enterprises (SMEs), are also identified.

The second step is to provide qualitative commentary on the ex ante risk reduction and risk financing mechanisms in place. This includes looking both at provisions made at the sovereign and subsovereign level, and the extent to which insurance solutions are adopted across different groups in society.

The third step compares the gap between these two steps, to provide a quantified assessment of the "protection gap." Specifically, this involves an estimate of the proportion of losses that might be covered by insurance solutions plus quantitative assessment of the adequacy of risk retention mechanisms to cover losses from floods and earthquakes. In the context of Figure 1, it compares the height of the blue bar with the height of the ex ante measures box. The results are presented in two ways: first, the extent to which AALs are covered by risk retention and risk transfer solutions. Second, it looks at the return period of flood and earthquake events that, when accounting for the losses that might be insured, would cause the risk retention mechanisms in the country to be exhausted.

These are then examined in three different ways: first, by assuming that the risk retention mechanisms need to cover both the uninsured direct losses and indirect losses. Second, by assuming that risk retention mechanisms need to cover only the uninsured direct losses that events might cause; and third, assuming that risk retention mechanisms need to cover the emergency response costs associated with different events.[8]

The fourth step looks at the extent to which other sources of finance may allow governments, households, and businesses to meet the financial costs or losses caused by disaster events. At the sovereign level, this involves an examination of the macroeconomic context of the country and, where data is available, its financial response to previous disaster events. In particular, this determines the ease with which governments may be able to access borrowing to cover the costs or losses of a disaster event. At the level of households and businesses, the assessment is predominantly carried out through a review of the extent of financial inclusion in the country, which provides a proxy for their ease of accessing finance. This is complemented by an assessment of social protection provision, recognizing that social protection is often an essential way for vulnerable individuals and households to cope with disaster events,[9] while recognizing that such mechanisms will also increase contingent liabilities at the sovereign level.

The final step of the analysis provides a summary of the key insights for each country and the implications for involvement in a regional risk transfer facility.

---

[8] It is assumed that emergency response costs are equal to 23% of the direct losses of a flood event and 16% of the direct losses of an earthquake event, based on industry practice derived from an analysis of historic events. Insurance penetration is not taken into account when assessing the extent to which risk retention will cover emergency response costs.

[9] World Bank. 2019. *Social Protection and Disaster Recovery*. https://www.gfdrr.org/sites/default/files/publication/Social_Protection_Guidance_Note_FINAL.pdf.

3 Results

Regional Trends

The protection gap for CAREC member countries varies materially but, in all cases, there appear to be important opportunities to improve the current approach. Table 1 depicts four (three substantive, one due to uncertainty) broad categories of CAREC member countries according to the estimated size of the protection gap. This is partly determined by reference to the quantified protection gap as set out in Figure 1 but also draws on a wider evidence base. Table 3 at the end of this section, summarizes this wider assessment. It illustrates for each country:

(i)   the estimated direct average annual losses caused by the combination of floods and earthquakes in each country, expressed as a % of gross national income (GNI);

(ii) the estimated absolute amount and percentage of direct average annual losses that are not covered by ex ante mechanisms;

(iii) the expected number of fatalities each year from flood and earthquake events;

(iv) the estimated frequency and severity of both flood and earthquake events (measured in terms of return period) that would exhaust the ex ante mechanisms. This is presented in three different ways, assuming that ex ante measures are expected to cover: both direct and indirect losses, ex ante direct losses only, and ex ante recovery (but not reconstruction) costs of different events;

(v)   the macroeconomic context in each country and the extent that the government is likely to easily and quickly access debt to recover from disaster events; and

(vi) the extent to which (vulnerable) individuals and households are expected to have access to financial resources to recover from disaster events, taking into account both levels of financial inclusion and the provision of social protection.

The largest protection gap is found in the **critically insufficient financing group,** including Afghanistan, Pakistan, and Tajikistan. The extent of ex ante risk finance measures is very limited, with a large proportion of AALs not covered by existing ex ante mechanisms. Even very frequent and lower severity events are likely to exhaust any risk retention mechanisms. The challenges in these countries are compounded by low sovereign credit ratings[10] and low rates of financial inclusion of households. Moreover, in all three countries, the provinces where risk and vulnerability coincide most strongly are characterized by a heavy reliance on agriculture and basic agro-processing, largely undertaken by smallholder farmers and SMEs. In Afghanistan, this includes Herat, Badakhshan, and Nangarhar; in Pakistan, Sindh is a notable hot spot, while in Tajikistan, the greatest problems are likely to be in Khatlon. In Tajikistan and Pakistan, flooding requires the greatest financing need, whereas in Afghanistan, earthquakes are a greater challenge.

There is an urgent need to enhance all aspects of the disaster risk finance landscape for these countries. Strategies should be developed at the sovereign and the household level, and for common events (where risk retention is often more appropriate) and rarer events (where risk transfer is often more appropriate). The ability to pay for additional disaster risk finance will, remain an ongoing, foundational challenge.

---

[10]   Afghanistan currently does not have a credit rating.

Table 1: Country Protection Gap Classification

Group Name	Countries
Critically insufficient financing (85% or more of AALs from floods and earthquakes are not covered by ex ante mechanisms) and particularly weak macroeconomic context	Afghanistan Pakistan Tajikistan
Weak financing (~0%–85% of AALs not covered by ex ante mechanisms)*	Kyrgyz Republic Mongolia Uzbekistan
Modest financing (AALs from flood and earthquakes are covered)	Azerbaijan Georgia Kazakhstan
Insufficient data or beyond the scope of this study	PRC, Inner Mongolia Autonomous Region PRC, Xinjiang Uygur Autonomous Region Turkmenistan

AALs = average annual losses, PRC = People's Republic of China.

[*] The analysis finds that the ex ante mechanisms in Mongolia are just large enough to cover the AALs associated with flood and earthquake events. However, it is placed in this category due to its qualitatively different macroeconomic content to the countries in the Modest Financing group and because analysis of past events suggests that not all ex ante finance budgeted for disaster events has been used for this purpose. Similarly, Uzbekistan is placed in this group of countries despite having a large proportion (85%) of its AALs unfunded on account of its stronger macroeconomic context than the countries in the critically insufficient category.

Source: Consultant team modeling.

The **weak financing group** includes the Kyrgyz Republic, Mongolia, and Uzbekistan. These countries all implement some risk retention mechanisms and have greater financial resilience to the most common disaster events than countries in the first group. Both the sovereign governments and households are also somewhat more likely to be able to access borrowing than countries in the first group.

The context across these three countries also differs in important ways. The Kyrgyz Republic is expected to see the largest losses of any country in the CAREC region as a percentage of GNI, due to both extensive flood and earthquake risk. At the household level, there are particular challenges with financial inclusion rates declining sharply outside the capital city, Bishkek. Risk and vulnerability coincide most notably in Jalal-Abad and Osh. In both provinces, agricultural production is important, especially of horticultural products, while in Jalal-Abad, in particular, this is complemented by a number of medium-sized enterprises in the industrial sector including in textile and leather manufacturing, construction, and confectionery.

In Mongolia, flood risk is substantially more important than earthquake risk, while the overall level of risk is lower than in many other CAREC countries. Compared to other countries in the region, there is likely to be a particular value in supporting sovereign arrangements. By contrast, challenges at the household level are mitigated by moderate insurance penetration and higher levels of financial inclusion than seen in other countries in the region. Social protection measures are well targeted to support the most vulnerable. Risk and vulnerability overlap most acutely in Khuvsgul, where livestock herding is the principal economic activity.

Uzbekistan faces somewhat more risk from floods than from earthquakes. While the proportion of its AALs that is not covered by risk retention mechanisms is high, recent economic development provides stronger macroeconomic fundamentals than the other countries in this group. The pace and extent of this development have been uneven, and measures of financial inclusion have been declining. Subnational analysis suggests that risk and vulnerability may combine most notably in Andijan and Namangan. Economic activity in these provinces comprises of a combination of agriculture and industrial manufacturing and trade, with SMEs accounting for much of this activity.

The **modest financing** group of countries consists of Azerbaijan, Georgia, and Kazakhstan. All three of these countries have reasonably good access to finance to help respond to disaster events. A further common feature of these countries is that the provinces where risk and vulnerability coincide rely less heavily on agriculture than similar regions in the other groupings with, instead, activities such as light manufacturing accounting for a relatively larger proportion of economic activity (e.g., Aran in Azerbaijan, Kvemo Kartli in Georgia, and Turkestan in Kazakhstan). A further hot spot is in Kyzylorda in Kazakhstan where fossil fuel extraction is important. Existing risk retention mechanisms are sufficient to help cover the emergency response costs of the most frequent events. However, at present, the direct losses of a 1 in 10-year flood event in either country would exhaust current risk retention mechanisms, rising, respectively, to a 1 in 100-year and 1 in 25-year earthquake event. As such, the greatest need and opportunity for this group may be for risk transfer instruments that support reconstruction costs for events of this threshold of severity or greater (e.g., a Contingent Disaster Financing Facility).

The final group is where data are insufficient, or the required assessment goes beyond the scope of this study. This includes Inner Mongolia Autonomous Region (IMAR) and Xinjiang Uygur Autonomous Region (XUAR) in the People's Republic of China (PRC), and Turkmenistan. Lack of data prevented the analysis from being conducted for Turkmenistan. In the case of XUAR and IMAR, the extent of support received from central government depends on the national context.[11] This requires an assessment of the flood and earthquake risk in the rest of the country, which is beyond the scope of this study.

Implications of Analysis for a Regional Risk Transfer Facility

This technical assistance (TA) targets the development of a regional risk transfer facility, to strengthen the available tools for governments to address and finance disaster risk. The quantification of the protection gap is an essential activity, by estimating the need for risk financing on an individual country basis, as well as regionally. The risk transfer facility could provide sustainably priced insurance capacity, with all CAREC member countries eligible.

Risk financing on a regional basis (or risk pooling) is powerful. As stressed in section 2, such facilities permit members to harness the benefits of risk diversification and improve the economies of scale in seeking private sector risk transfer. This increases the financial efficiency and the affordability of insurance. This is accentuated if the regional facility is well capitalized, perhaps utilizing development bank finance, by also providing price stability, particularly after a loss event, being less exposure to insurance market shocks. These structural changes thereby reduce the total cost of disaster risk for CAREC member countries, underlying the benefits of regional collaboration.

The benefits are also more than financial. A facility can become a focus for regional cooperation on risk understanding, modeling, management, and wider scientific engagement. The facility offers a voice in the operation and direction of the scheme, putting the current, future, and changing needs of member countries at the center of its offering.

Risk pooling does, however, require careful design. As the facility will pool the disaster risk of all members, regional collaboration is essential for a credible, sustainable facility. The facility must be based upon accurate and transparent risk quantification and fair premium pricing with no cross-subsidization. First, the facility must offer risk financing solutions that meet the needs of member countries to ensure commitment. Second, the facility's portfolio must be well-balanced to ensure the disaster risk admitted to the pool does not dominate and potentially adversely affect the risk transfer cost of another member. Third, efforts to reduce risk over time are required such that risk financing costs do not continue to grow in line with that of the value at risk and the expected intensification of rainfall extremes.

---

[11]   If XUAR and IMAR were the only provinces in the PRC that faced material earthquake and flood risk then the amount of centralized support would be easily sufficient to cover these risks. By contrast, if the earthquake and flood risk in all other provinces was materially greater than in XUAR and IMAR then the amount of central government support might not be sufficient to fully cover the risks in these provinces.

The protection gap assessment helps inform these considerations. The average annual loss as a percentage of GNI illustrates the quantum of disaster risk faced by each country. Understanding the frequency with which risk retention and transfer mechanisms are exhausted is directly informative for the services to be offered by the facility to help countries reduce the frequency with which arrangements are exhausted. This is equally true of the emergency response cost adequacy assessment.[12] Furthermore, the analysis for each country is deliberately consistent, to ensure fairness in the conclusions and implications of the analysis.

Importantly, the protection gap assessment confirms the need for improved disaster risk financing. All CAREC member countries would benefit from a deeper, more extensive set of disaster risk financing tools. Although several countries have reserves to finance AALs—which should be a minimum policy objective—the estimated deficits in Afghanistan, the Kyrgyz Republic, Pakistan, Tajikistan, and Uzbekistan are particularly sizable.

The role of a regional risk transfer facility is accentuated by the generally low credit rating of CAREC member countries. This reduces a government's ability to secure loans at affordable rates, such as those post-disaster to help finance recovery and reconstruction. The cost benefits of arranging ex ante financing are larger when credit ratings are weak. Countries with weak credit ratings should explore the full range of financing options, given the high cost of financing post event. This includes contingent disaster financing, which may be available from development banks. They are also likely to particularly benefit from a regional risk transfer facility, which can deliver financing in a low-cost, sustainable, donor-friendly manner.

By grouping countries with common challenges, it potentially becomes easier to identify common solutions. This might inform the countries who participate in the pilot phase of the facility. While the groupings identified in this report derive only from an assessment of similar risk financing needs, they could permit a facility to offer a similar product to the countries, safe in the knowledge that this would fill a risk transfer need in each. Examples of potential policies to be issued from the CAREC facility are illustrated in Table 2. For example, the critically insufficient financing group of countries would likely benefit from an emergency response cover attaching at a 1 in 5-year flood. This is similar to policies issued by the African Risk Capacity in Africa for drought. The weak financing group of countries could instead seek a cover at a 1 in 20-year level, given the extent of current reserves and financing arrangements. This again is likely to be even higher for the modest financing group, with risk transfer more likely to be sought at the 1 in 50-year or higher level, commensurate with a major flood or earthquake event.

Each member country will purchase an insurance policy from the facility company, tailored to their risk profile, stated needs, and demands. A common pricing methodology would be employed for all contracts, reflecting the risk they bring to the pool. As illustrated, member countries will have different demand for products. Emergency response products that protect at a 1 in 5-year level pay more frequently than those attaching at the 1 in 50-year level. Policies that pay more frequently will cost more per unit of cover than those that pay less often. Materially different policies, and so expectations and costs, may increase the challenges of building confidence and commitment in the pilot phase of the facility.

This does not mean pilot countries for the regional facility may only be drawn from the groupings developed in this report. These groupings provide important information on the likely needs for, and expectations from risk financing. For example, in a pilot regional facility with two countries from the Critical Insufficient Financing group and one country from the Modest Financing group, the objectives of the latter are likely to be different. Countries across groupings are highly similar on some risks. However, the grouping process in this report is designed to account for more than just the design of a regional facility and thus should not be used as a rigid guide.

---

[12]   Indeed, the emergency response analysis was informed by other sovereign disaster risk transfer facilities (e.g., Caribbean Catastrophe Risk Insurance Facility [CCRIF SPC] and the African Risk Capacity), which provide emergency response insurance, indicating the potential utility to CAREC member countries.

Table 2: Emergency Response Insurance Product Options

Group Name	Countries	Flood Emergency Response Product	Earthquake Emergency Response Product
Critically insufficient financing	Afghanistan Pakistan Tajikistan	1 in 5-year	1 in 5-year
Weak financing	Kyrgyz Republic Mongolia Uzbekistan	1 in 20-year	1 in 25-year
Modest financing	Azerbaijan Georgia Kazakhstan	1 in 50-year	1 in 200-year
Insufficient data or beyond the scope of this study	PRC, IMAR PRC, XUAR Turkmenistan	NA	NA

NA = not available, IMAR = Inner Mongolia Autonomous Region, PRC = People's Republic of China, XUAR = Xinjiang Uygur Autonomous Region.

Source: Consultant team modeling.

All CAREC member countries would benefit from additional risk financing, and facilities such as the Caribbean Catastrophe Risk Insurance Facility (CCRIF) show that a mix of small, large, developed, and developing countries, with different risk appetites can all be accommodated. The key is to ensure no single country's risk dominates the pool and that premiums can be seen to fairly represent the risk that each country brings to the facility. Further, the size of economies and disaster risk is not perfectly balanced in each group. Typically, facilities manage their exposure to ensure that no one country predominates by limiting cover that can be purchased to a maximum amount and by use of reinsurance. CCRIF, for example, originally imposed a $50 million cover cap (now lifted as the facility has grown). CCRIF's pricing formula also charges more for those countries that contribute most to the need for reinsurance. As such, the groups identified in this analysis should not be considered as definitive, but instead are aimed at facilitating discussion, to start building consensus on the design of the pilot regional facility.

Table 3: Summary of Protection Gap Analysis

Country	AAL as % of GNI[a]	Unfunded AAL, ($, %)	Average annual human losses from flood and earthquakes		Event frequency where direct and indirect loss, less (assumed) insured losses, exceed existing ex ante risk retention		Event frequency where direct loss, less (assumed) insured losses, exceed existing ex ante risk retention		Event frequency where estimated emergency response costs exceed current risk retention mechanisms		Macroeconomic context and ability for sovereign to borrow	Ability of individuals and households to access resources after an event
			Flood	EQ	Flood	EQ	Flood	EQ	Flood	EQ		
Afghanistan	0.14	118 million, 99%	66	125	All	All	All	All	All	All	Extremely challenging, very limited access to debt markets	Low rates of financial inclusion with high gender inequality and limited social protection.
Azerbaijan	0.09	AAL covered	3	48	1 in 25	1 in 20	1 in 50	1 in 25	>1 in 200	>1 in 200	Strong with close-to-investment grade credit rating. Medium-term structural challenges.	Financial inclusion relatively low and concentrated among higher income groups in Baku. Limited social protection.
Georgia	0.08	AAL covered	165	11	1 in 5	1 in 20	1 in 5	1 in 25	1 in 200	1 in 200	Moderate. Improving before COVID-19 crisis. Credit rating higher than most others in region	High rates of financial inclusion and generous social protection. Inequalities by region and age group.
Kazakhstan	0.11	AAL covered	392	42	1 in 10	1 in 75	1 in 10	1 in 100	>1 in 200	>1 in 200	Only country other than the PRC with investment grade credit rating. Medium-term structural challenges.	Relatively high financial inclusion but with inequality across income groups. Social protection measures not well-targeted
Kyrgyz Republic	0.44	81 million, 56%	193	27	1 in 5	1 in 10	1 in 5	1 in 10	1 in 20	1 in 25	Credit rating median with CAREC region. Moderate risk of debt distress	Financial inclusion concentrated in capital. Relatively supportive social protection
Mongolia	0.07	AAL covered[b]	92	1	1 in 10	>1 in 200	1 in 10	>1 in 200	1 in 20	>1 in 200	Moderate to weak. External debt: GDP among highest in CAREC, low credit rating	High rates of financial inclusion and significant social protection

continued on next page

Table 3: continued

Country	AAL as % of GNI[a]	Unfunded AAL ($, %)	Average annual human losses from flood and earthquakes		Event frequency where direct and indirect loss, less (assumed) insured losses, exceed existing ex ante risk retention		Event frequency where direct loss, less (assumed) insured losses, exceed existing ex ante risk retention		Event frequency where estimated emergency response costs exceed current risk retention mechanisms		Macroeconomic context and ability for sovereign to borrow	Ability of individuals and households to access resources after an event
			Flood	EQ	Flood	EQ	Flood	EQ	Flood	EQ		
Pakistan	0.20	2.1 billion, 97%	234	863	All	All	All	All	All	All	Weak position. High risk of debt distress and second lowest credit rating in region.	Very low rates of financial inclusion. Social protection also limited but with innovations.
PRC, IMAR	0.09	NA	8	40	NA	NA	NA	NA	NA	NA	Unclear but potentially weak at the province level. Robust national financing arrangements.	Statistics not comparable to rest of CAREC but likely to be moderate–high
PRC, XUAR	0.12	NA	5	84	NA	NA	NA	NA	NA	NA	Unclear but potentially weak at the province level. Robust national financing arrangements.	Statistics not comparable to rest of CAREC but likely to be moderate–high
Tajikistan	0.32	107 million, 86%	45	37	1 in 5	1 in 5	1 in 5	1 in 5	1 in 5	1 in 10	Weak position. High risk of debt distress and third lowest credit rating.	Growing financial inclusion but still lower than many other countries in region. Low and poorly targeted social protection.
Turkmenistan	0.18	NA	173	7	NA	NA	NA	NA	NA	NA	Limited access to international debt markets	Growing financial inclusion but still lower other countries in region.
Uzbekistan	0.24	512 million, 84%	219	92	1 in 2	1 in 10	1 in 2	1 in 10	1 in 5	1 in 20	Moderate–strong but short-term challenges from COVID-19.	Declining financial inclusion and limited social assistance.

AAL = average annual loss, B = billion, CAREC = Central Asia Regional Economic Cooperation, COVID-19 = coronavirus disease, EQ = earthquake, GDP = gross domestic product, GNI = gross national income, IMAR = Inner Mongolia Autonomous Region, NA = not available, PRC = People's Republic of China, XUAR = Xinjiang Uygur Autonomous Region.

[a] GNI data (GNI in current international $) used to take account of the importance of remittances in many parts of the CAREC region. GNI data taken from World Development Indicators. GDP used for IMAR and XUAR where province level GNI data is not available drawing from press reports.

[b] Note that, for consistency with the analytical approach taken in other countries, it is assumed that all of the reserve funds in Mongolia are available for covering the costs/losses associated with flood and earthquake events. However, when events have occurred historically, the funds in these reserves have not always been used for this purpose.

Source: Consultant team modeling.

Afghanistan

Flood and Earthquake Risk

Figure 3 presents exceedance probability[13] curves for flood and earthquake risk created for this TA. Consistent with these exceedance probability curves, AALs for floods are around $62 million (rising to $74 million when indirect losses are included) and $57 million for earthquake (rising to $76 million when including indirect losses). As is typical, most of the AALs associated with flood risk are expected from relatively frequent events, while most of the AALs associated with earthquakes are the result of less frequent, more severe events. The AAL from flood and earthquake combined, excluding indirect losses, amounts to around 0.14% of 2019 GNI in the country.[14]

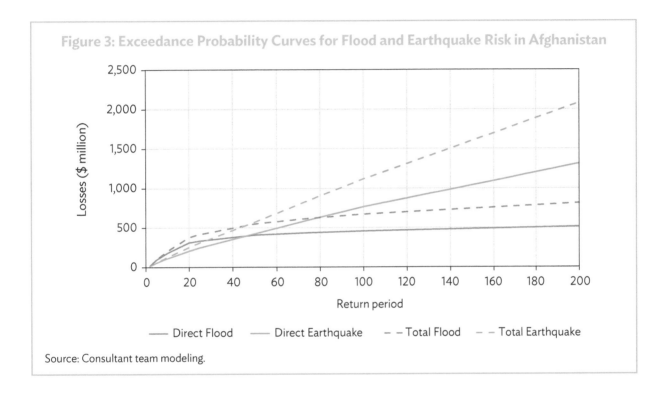

Figure 3: Exceedance Probability Curves for Flood and Earthquake Risk in Afghanistan

Source: Consultant team modeling.

There are also significant human losses associated with flood and earthquake risks. The modeling analysis suggests that, on average, 125 people die from earthquakes each year in Afghanistan, the second-highest number of any country in the region, and 66 people from floods. The average number of people severely affected by earthquakes and floods each year exceed 57,000 and 42,000, respectively.[15] Both human and financial losses arise in a country that already faces complex development challenges. Building on an analysis to guide the allocation of the COVID-19 donor support

13 An exceedance probability curve plots the relationship between the return period of event(s) and the losses and/or costs of events. It is referred to as an exceedance probability curve as a return period can be reinterpreted in terms of the probability that the losses of event(s) of that size in that time period will be exceeded. For example, there is a 1% chance of suffering losses greater than those associated with a 1 in 100-year event. All exceedance probability curves in this analysis are annual exceedance probability curves, reflecting losses from all events within a year (rather than occurrence exceedance probability curves that reflect losses from the largest event within a year).

14 Except where stated, GNI reported in current international dollars using purchasing power parity exchange rates.

15 The number of people severely affected by earthquakes is the population that can be expected to witness earthquake-caused ground-shaking of Intensity Index VIII on the Modified Mercalli Intensity Scale, defined as "Damage slight in specially designed structures. Considerable damage in ordinary substantial buildings with partial collapse. Damage great in poorly built structures. Fall of chimneys, factory stacks, columns, monuments, walls. Heavy furniture overturned." The number of people severely affected by floods is the number of people living in premises subject to a flood depth of 1 meter or more.

packages that provided food packages and direct cash transfers to households and communities, a 2021 analysis identified that 76% of the population, or an estimated 30.5 million people (14.9 million female and 15.6 million male), are currently in need of social assistance to prevent them slipping into or into worsening humanitarian need.[16]

Looking at the intra-country variation in risks, both expected loss of life and average annual financial loss are heavily concentrated in Kabul. Relatively speaking, poverty challenges in Kabul are less acute than in other provinces in the country. However, there are a number of "hot spot" provinces where losses are relatively high, and measures of poverty are particularly acute. These include Herat (where flood risk is particularly prominent), Badakhshan (where earthquake risk is pronounced) and Nangarhar (where flood and earthquake risk are broadly equivalent in impact). A similar pattern emerges when looking at risk in terms of expected loss of life. Figure 4 provides more detail.

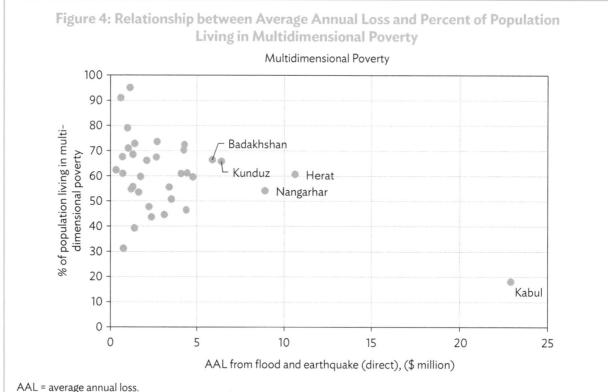

Figure 4: Relationship between Average Annual Loss and Percent of Population Living in Multidimensional Poverty

AAL = average annual loss.

Note: Multidimensional poverty measures poverty by capturing deprivations in health, education, and living standards that a person faces simultaneously.

Sources: Consultant team modeling and Oxford Poverty and Human Development Initiative.

In these provinces, agriculture and agro-processing are the dominant economic activities. These will be largely or exclusively undertaken by SMEs. Key agricultural production includes saffron, pistachios, cashmere, wool, and poppies. Wheat is also particularly important in Badakhshan and Nangarhar. Agro-processing activities include honey-extraction, and olive oil and sunflower oil manufacture. In Jalal–Abad, the capital of Nangarhar, there are some small-scale factories in soap-making and marble.[17]

---

[16]   United Nations Office for the Coordination of Humanitarian Affairs. 2021. *Humanitarian Needs Overview: Afghanistan*. https://reliefweb.int/sites/reliefweb.int/files/resources/afghanistan_humanitarian_needs_overview_2021_0.pdf.

[17]   Islamic Republic of Afghanistan, Central Statistical Office. 2016. *Socio-Demographic and Economic Survey 2016 Herat*. https://afghanistan.unfpa.org/sites/default/files/pub-pdf/SDES_HERAT_FINAL_ENG.pdf; GRM. 2006. *Provincial Profile: Badakhshan*. https://www.ecoi.net/en/file/local/1338833/432_1197541686_badakhshan-20provincial-20profile.pdf; GRM. 2006. *Provincial Profile: Nangarhar*. https://www.ecoi.net/en/file/local/1048565/1222_1197554805_nangarhar-provincial-profile.pdf.

Risk Retention and Insurance Penetration

As of July 2021, there are no government budgeted risk retention mechanisms in Afghanistan. Historically, the central government allocated funding for disasters to a National Emergency Fund (through Code 91). This fund was used for both disaster relief and response as well as preparedness and mitigation, with the funds allocated upon recommendation by the Afghanistan National Disaster Management Authority. However, no budget is being allocated through this code as of July 2021, due to the fiscal deficit and alternative spending priorities.

The main source of "on-demand" funding in response to disaster events is provided through the donor-funded Afghanistan Humanitarian Fund. This is managed by the Humanitarian Financing Unit of the United Nations Office for the Coordination of Humanitarian Affairs. This has two allocation modalities, one of which is "to enable rapid and flexible allocation of funds in the event of unforeseen emergencies, or to address acute gaps." In 2019, out of all funding provided by the Afghanistan Humanitarian Fund, $44.6 million out of $63.9 million (70%) was allocated through this modality.[18]

Similarly, the insurance market in Afghanistan is underdeveloped. The first private insurance company was founded in 2007, and the market is generally targeted toward expat-oriented, niche industries such as mining, construction, nongovernment organizations (NGOs), and embassies.[19] Property insurance penetration in 2016 (premiums for property insurance as a percentage of GDP) is estimated at 0.13%,[20] with coverage being almost exclusively for industrial or commercial properties, rather than family households. There is no history of flood insurance or evidence to suggest that losses from floods are insured, despite frequent deaths and property damage due to flash flooding. Nor is there any agricultural insurance.

Quantification of the Protection Gap

Based on the modeling undertaken in this assessment, AALs associated with earthquakes and floods are estimated to be $119 million per annum. The average annual costs associated with emergency response to disaster events is estimated to be around $23 million. It is assumed that no risk retention mechanisms are in place to meet any of these costs or losses.[21] Based on the low insurance penetration, the analysis assumes that around 1% of the losses from earthquakes and floods might be insured.[22]

The net result is that the protection gap is substantial and that almost all losses associated with flood and earthquakes would need to be met through ex post measures. Figure 5 shows that the average protection gap (the residual AAL after accounting for risk retention and risk transfer) is around $118 million. Table 4 shows that as of July 2021, existing funding is insufficient to cover the total losses, the direct losses, or even the emergency response costs associated with events of all frequencies.

---

[18] Afghanistan Humanitarian Fund. 2020. *2019 Annual Report.* https://www.unocha.org/sites/unocha/files/Afghanistan%20Humanitarian%20Fund%20%20Annual%20Report%202019_final%20100120.pdf.

[19] Insurance Nexus Global Trend Map. 2017. https://www.the-digital-insurer.com/wp-content/uploads/2018/04/1156-Insurance-Nexus-Global-Trend-Map.pdf.

[20] Based on data provided by Willis Towers Watson (2020).

[21] The resources provided by the Afghanistan Humanitarian Fund is excluded from the analysis as it reflects funding provided by donors and may not be a sustainable source of financing into the medium term.

[22] There is no direct data available on the percentage of properties insured against different risks. The assumption that 1% of losses might be covered by insurance is informed by a calculation of the estimated property insurance premiums, given by market reports at around $2.6 million, expressed as a percentage of earthquake and flood AALs. This ratio is then calibrated to estimates of insured losses in other countries where more information is available. See discussion in section 2 and annex.

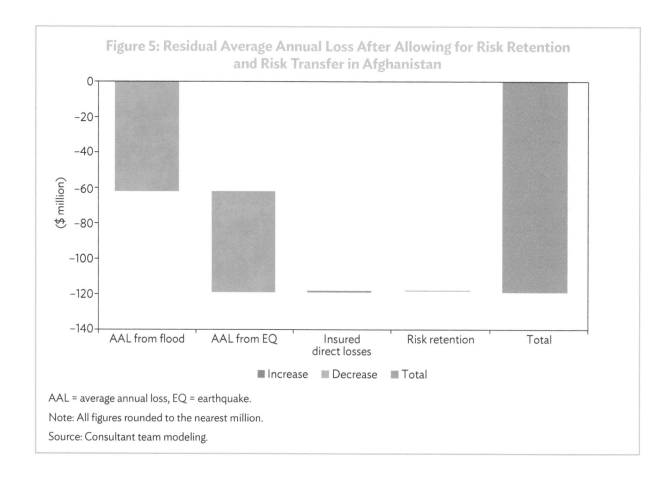

Figure 5: Residual Average Annual Loss After Allowing for Risk Retention and Risk Transfer in Afghanistan

AAL = average annual loss, EQ = earthquake.

Note: All figures rounded to the nearest million.

Source: Consultant team modeling.

Table 4: Event Frequency at which Ex Ante Mechanisms Are Exhausted in Afghanistan

Event frequency where direct and indirect loss, less (assumed) insured losses, exceed existing ex ante risk retention		Event frequency where direct loss, less (assumed) insured losses, exceed existing ex ante risk retention		Event frequency where estimated emergency response costs exceed current risk retention mechanisms	
Flood	**Earthquake**	**Flood**	**Earthquake**	**Flood**	**Earthquake**
All	All	All	All	All	All

Source: Consultant team modeling.

Ability to Rely on Ex Post Borrowing

A 2020 International Monetary Fund (IMF) analysis marked Afghanistan as being at high risk of external debt distress.[23] This has been exacerbated by the COVID-19 crisis with domestic activity slowing sharply and disruptions in trade and transport affecting Afghanistan's narrow export base. In the first quarter of 2020, government revenue fell by 10% compared to 2019, and the fiscal deficit increased to 2.5% of GDP.[24] Figure 6 summarizes macroeconomic data from Afghanistan as of July 2021.

---

[23]   International Monetary Fund (IMF). 2020. *Islamic Republic of Afghanistan. Request for Disbursement under the Rapid Credit Facility – Debt Sustainability Analysis.* https://www.elibrary.imf.org/view/journals/002/2020/143/article-A002-en.xml.

[24]   M. A. Kose, S. Kurlat, F. Ohnsorge, and N. Sugawara. 2017. A Cross-Country Database of Fiscal Space. *Policy Research Working Paper* 8157. Washington, DC: World Bank. https://www.worldbank.org/en/research/brief/fiscal-space.

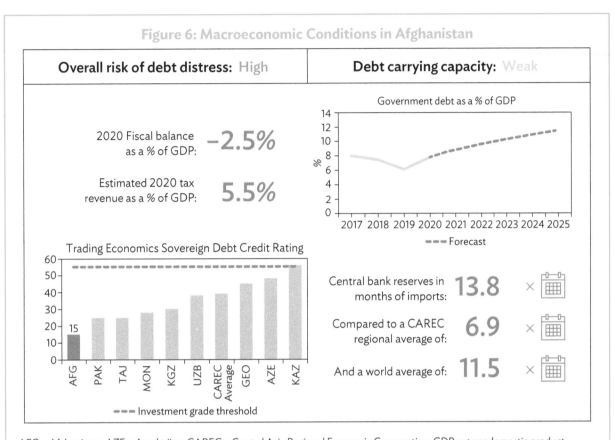

Figure 6: Macroeconomic Conditions in Afghanistan

Overall risk of debt distress: High

Debt carrying capacity: Weak

2020 Fiscal balance as a % of GDP: **−2.5%**

Estimated 2020 tax revenue as a % of GDP: **5.5%**

Government debt as a % of GDP

--- Forecast

Trading Economics Sovereign Debt Credit Rating

--- Investment grade threshold

Central bank reserves in months of imports: **13.8** ×

Compared to a CAREC regional average of: **6.9** ×

And a world average of: **11.5** ×

AFG = Afghanistan, AZE = Azerbaijan, CAREC = Central Asia Regional Economic Cooperation, GDP = gross domestic product, GEO = Georgia, KAZ = Kazakhstan, KGZ = Kyrgyz Republic, MON = Mongolia, PAK = Pakistan, TAJ = Tajikistan, UZB = Uzbekistan.

Sources: World Bank Open Data https://data.worldbank.org/, IMF World Economic Outlook Database. https://www.imf.org/en/Data, and Trading Economics. https://tradingeconomics.com/ (accessed May 2021).

Most households do not have the ability to access finance to help respond to disaster events. As of July 2021, Afghanistan had one of the lowest rates of financial inclusion in the world with just 15% of the adult (over 15) population owning a bank account, and only 4% having saved at a financial institution. These obstacles are even more pronounced for women. Only 7% of Afghan women have a bank account, compared with 23% for men. There is a similar divide in terms of the proportion of people saving at a financial institution with 4% of men but only 1% of women reported as having savings accounts.[25]

In response to these challenges, national and international NGOs have supported the creation of self-help groups to support household financial management. Self-help groups are voluntary (financial) saving associations comprised of local community members who come together at regular intervals (weekly, biweekly, or monthly) and contribute a small amount of money collectively (for example AF20, AF50 or AF100 per person) to a communal fund. This money is kept in a saving box, recorded in a ledger, and can be loaned out to members of the group with agreed upon conditions. The program was initiated by Afghan Aid in 2004 and supported by other NGOs and multilateral organizations including Aga Khan Foundation, CARE, UN Habitat, Mission East, and Oxfam. Reviews have found that this approach has been effective among the individuals it reaches, especially women.[26]

[25]   The Global Findex Database. 2017 (accessed May 2021). https://globalfindex.worldbank.org/.

[26]   A. Schmeding. 2018. *The Self-Help Group Approach in Afghanistan.* https://reliefweb.int/sites/reliefweb.int/files/resources/AFG_self%20help%20group_study.pdf.

Summary

Afghanistan is in a weak position in financing disaster losses. It faces annual losses from flood and earthquakes that sum to more than $118 million per year, in a country that already faces substantial humanitarian and development challenges. There are no explicit ex ante risk retention mechanisms, while the insurance market is very immature. Most of its citizens are not in a position to access the sums of finance needed to respond to disaster events, instead having to rely almost exclusively on humanitarian support.

Azerbaijan

Flood and Earthquake Risk

Figure 7 provides the estimated exceedance probability curves for flood and earthquake risk in Azerbaijan. Earthquake risk is somewhat greater than flood risk across the country, with an AAL for earthquake of around $71 million (rising to $85 million when taking account indirect losses) and for flood $58 million, rising to $67 million with indirect losses included. The sum of the AALs for the two hazards is over $129 million, rising to $152 million with indirect losses included. The AAL from direct losses is equivalent to 0.09% of 2019 GNI, which is the 10th highest figure as a proportion of GNI in the CAREC region.

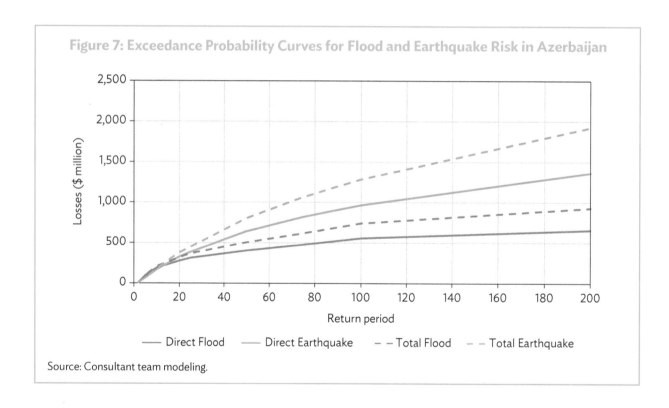

Figure 7: Exceedance Probability Curves for Flood and Earthquake Risk in Azerbaijan

Source: Consultant team modeling.

The relative importance of earthquake risk is also clear in the modeling results on expected loss of life. The modeling analysis suggests that the average number of lives lost per year to earthquakes is 48, the fourth highest among CAREC countries. By contrast, only three lives are expected to be lost each year to floods, the lowest of all CAREC countries. However, when considering the number of people severely affected by the two perils, the contrast is less stark with just over 12,000 people expected to be severely affected by earthquakes and over 10,000 expected to be severely affected by floods.

Within the country, interregional data on the Human Development Index (HDI) shows little variation, with all regions for which there is data having an HDI score of between 0.70 and 0.80. Nonetheless, the Aran region stands out. It is expected to see both the largest loss of lives from flood and earthquake, the largest AAL from floods and the largest AAL from flood and earthquakes combined. It also records the second-lowest HDI score[27] of any region for which data is available. Figure 8 provides more detail. In 2009, this region accounted for around 21% of the individual entrepreneurs in the country and 15% of the SMEs (in both cases, the second-highest percentage after the capital, Baku)[28] with important economic activities including cotton growing, mechanical engineering, light manufacturing, and construction materials.[29]

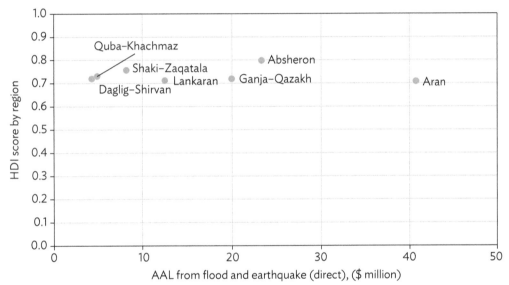

Figure 8: Relationship between Average Annual Loss and Human Development Index by Economic Regions in Azerbaijan

AAL = average annual loss.

Note: Nakhchivan and Kalbajar–Lachin excluded due to absence of Human Development Index data.

Source: Consultant team modeling and Global Data Lab.

27   The human development index aggregates information on life expectancy, education and per capita income and converts this to an index score of between 0 and 1 with scores closer to 1 representing higher levels of human development.
28   International Finance Corporation. 2009. *Study of Small and Medium Enterprises in Azerbaijan.* https://www.yumpu.com/en/document/read/22523990/study-of-small-and-medium-enterprises-in-azerbaijan-ifc.
29   Z. Aliyev. 2018. Modern Vacation of Economic Indicators of Caspian Regions in Azerbaijan. *Current Investigations in Agriculture and Current Research.* 1(4). https://lupinepublishers.com/agriculture-journal/fulltext/modern-vacation-of-economic-development-Indicators-of-caspian-regions-in-azerbaijan.ID.000119.php.

Risk Retention and Insurance Penetration

Azerbaijan has two key reserve funds that it can draw upon to support its response to disaster events.[30] The Reserve Fund of the President, which in the 2019 State Budget had around AZN300 million ($176 million); and the Reserve Fund of the State Budget, which in the 2019 State Budget had around AZN100 million ($59 million).

Azerbaijan's overall nonlife insurance rate in 2019—total insurance premiums divided by GDP—was 0.5%. Premiums for these policies, per capita, are $26. On this metric, Azerbaijan has broadly similar nonlife insurance penetration as Kazakhstan, Mongolia, and Turkmenistan.[31]

Azerbaijan law compels owners of real estate to purchase property insurance.[32] "Compulsory" property insurance has widened the coverage of households that are protected in the event of damage to their property. There has been steady growth of premiums associated with compulsory property insurance between 2017 and 2019 and a marked jumped in premiums collected in 2020. Press reports suggest that around 20%–25% of the potential compulsory market now takes out insurance.[33] However, while the compulsory coverage includes flood risk, earthquake cover is a voluntary add-on. According to insurance market reports, there is no information on the percentage of policies that include earthquake cover.

Insurance penetration is heavily concentrated in urban areas. Four times more urban than rural people possess any type of insurance policy, and there is a strong correlation between regional wealth and insurance penetration across the country. The largest areas of insurance penetration are based in Absheron and Daglig–Shirvan, the two wealthiest regions in Azerbaijan.[34] In 2015, on average, around 10% of people held an insurance policy (of any type), but this fell to only 3% when looking only at the rural population (footnote 33).

Quantification of the Protection Gap

The combined AAL for flood and earthquake risk in Azerbaijan is approximately $129 million. The inclusion of indirect losses increases this contingent liability to around $152 million although these indirect losses are excluded from the base-case calculations.

Of the direct losses, the base-case analysis assumes that 35% of direct flood losses in Absheron and Daglig–Shirvan and 10% of direct flood losses elsewhere in the country might be covered by insurance. Applying these percentages to the estimated exposure implies that 19.5% of the total exposure in the country was covered. This broadly aligns with market reports that suggest that compulsory property insurance had reached 12% of the population by 2012 and allowing for growth thereafter while at the same time considering that not all losses will be covered even when insurance is in place. For earthquake losses, which is not part of compulsory cover, the base-case analysis assumes 5% of direct losses in Absheron and Daglig–Shirvan and 1% of losses elsewhere in the country might be covered by insurance.

The analysis assumes that all funding in the Reserve Fund of the President and the Reserve Fund of the State Budget would be available to cover flood and earthquake risks if they materialized. On this basis, as Figure 9 shows, all the AAL for both floods and earthquakes could be covered. However, as Table 5 shows the impact of more

30   Government of Azerbaijan. The Law of the Republic of Azerbaijan: On the state budget of the Republic of Azerbaijan for 2019.
31   Data taken from Swiss Re Sigma. https://www.swissre.com/institute/research/sigma-research/World-insurance-series.html.
32   Compulsory Insurance Bureau. https://isb.az/en/.
33   M. Magnaval. 2020. Azerbaijan: Compulsory Real Estate Insurance Saw a Sharp Increase in 1Q 2020. https://www.xprimm.com/AZERBAIJAN-compulsory-real-estate-insurance-saw-a-sharp-increase-in-1Q2020-articol-2,12,39-15370.htm.
34   G. Ibadoghlu. 2018. Financial Inclusion, Financial Literacy and Financial Education in Azerbaijan. ADBI Working Paper Series. No. 842. Tokyo: ADBI. https://www.adb.org/sites/default/files/publication/421611/adbi-wp842.pdf.

extreme events might still cause financing challenges for the government, depending on the purpose of these funds. If the reserve funds were required to cover both the uninsured direct and indirect losses of disaster events, then they would be exhausted by the losses of a 1 in 25-year flood or a 1 in 20-year earthquake. For earthquakes, a 1 in 25-year event would lead to the reserves being exhausted even if there was a need to only cover the direct uninsured losses (but not indirect losses) whereas for floods, the reserves would be sufficient for a 1 in 50-year event. If the risk retention mechanisms are intended to only cover emergency response costs, then they would only be exhausted when covering the estimated emergency response costs of an event with a return period significantly greater than 1 in 200-years for both perils.

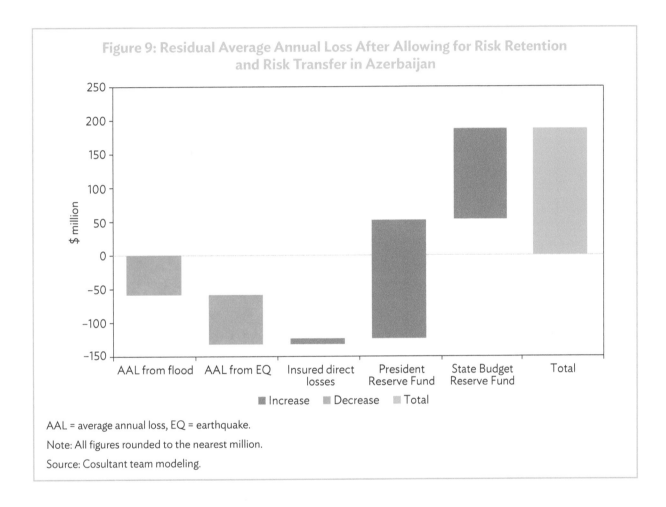

Figure 9: Residual Average Annual Loss After Allowing for Risk Retention and Risk Transfer in Azerbaijan

AAL = average annual loss, EQ = earthquake.

Note: All figures rounded to the nearest million.

Source: Cosultant team modeling.

Table 5: Event Frequency at which Ex Ante Mechanisms Are Exhausted in Azerbaijan

Event frequency where direct and indirect losses, less (assumed) insured losses, exceed existing ex ante risk retention		Event frequency where direct losses, less (assumed) insured losses, exceed existing ex ante risk retention		Event frequency where estimated emergency response costs exceed current risk retention mechanisms	
Flood	**Earthquake**	**Flood**	**Earthquake**	**Flood**	**Earthquake**
1 in 25	1 in 20	1 in 50	1 in 25	>1 in 200	>1 in 200

Source: Consultant team modeling.

Ability to Rely on Ex Post Borrowing

The current fiscal position of Azerbaijan is robust, although it is vulnerable to oil price shocks. Low public debt, an oil industry that enjoys a $15 per barrel break-even price,[35] and a large sovereign wealth fund with assets amounting to 82% of GDP means Azerbaijan has the financial resources to respond to many shocks and greater sovereign financial resilience than many other countries in the CAREC region. Consistent with this, it has a sovereign debt credit rating that is close to investment grade. However, while in 2018 the government ran a fiscal surplus of 8.4% of GDP, excluding the oil economy and associated revenue, the primary fiscal deficit amounted to 31.1% of non-oil GDP.[36] Some of this structural weakness has been exposed by the events of 2020 with the fiscal balance falling into a deficit of 6.4% of GDP. Figure 10 summarizes the key information related to Azerbaijan's current fiscal position.

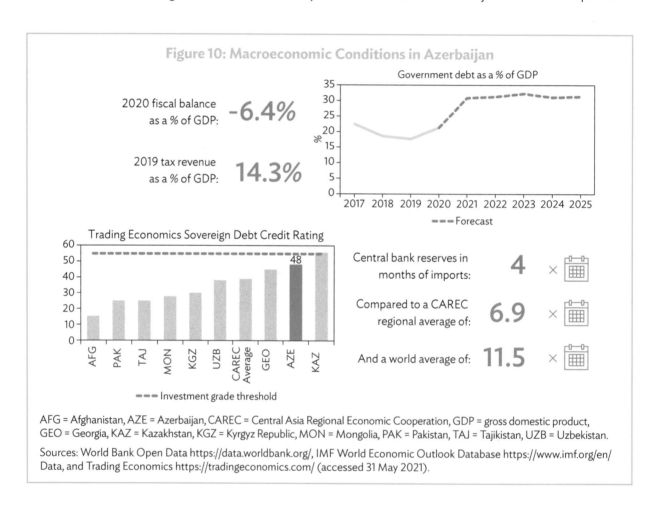

Figure 10: Macroeconomic Conditions in Azerbaijan

AFG = Afghanistan, AZE = Azerbaijan, CAREC = Central Asia Regional Economic Cooperation, GDP = gross domestic product, GEO = Georgia, KAZ = Kazakhstan, KGZ = Kyrgyz Republic, MON = Mongolia, PAK = Pakistan, TAJ = Tajikistan, UZB = Uzbekistan.

Sources: World Bank Open Data https://data.worldbank.org/, IMF World Economic Outlook Database https://www.imf.org/en/Data, and Trading Economics https://tradingeconomics.com/ (accessed 31 May 2021).

Consistent with this, the size of Azerbaijan's COVID-19 response measures (around $1600 million as of end May 2021) far exceeds the support that it has accessed from international development partners (around $207 million). Some of the difference was met by payments made out of the Reserve Fund of the President but most of the additional spending was financed through additional debt. The Government of Azerbaijan has also provided $5 million to the World Health Organization's strategic preparedness and response plan.[37]

[35] Fitch Ratings. 2020. *Fitch Affirms Azerbaijan at 'BB+'; Outlook Negative.* https://www.fitchratings.com/research/sovereigns/fitch-affirms-azerbaijan-at-bb-outlook-negative-17-07-2020.
[36] IMF. 2019. *Article IV Consultation.* https://www.imf.org/en/Publications/CR/Issues/2019/09/18/Republic-of-Azerbaijan-2019-Article-IV-Consultation-Press-Release-Staff-Report-and-Statement-48684.
[37] All data taken from the ADB COVID-19 policy database (accessed May 2021) https://covid19policy.adb.org/.

However, individual households' access to formal financial mechanisms to cope with the impact of disasters is more challenging. According to the 2017 Global Findex database, only 29% of the total population owns a bank account, with the majority of these based in the capital Baku. When only looking at the poorest 40% of the population, account ownership falls to 18%, reflecting inequality across income groups. Only 5% of the Azeri population saves at a financial institution, falling to 2% among the poorest two quintiles and among the rural population (footnote 24).

Moreover, the social protection mechanism is not currently designed to offer shock-responsive support to the Azeri population. The Azerbaijan 2020 Strategy states that *"the experience of recent years shows that in order to effectively fight natural disasters and their consequences, the state should prioritize relevant activities in emergencies and the establishment of rapid reaction mechanisms for the social security of the population in such situations."*[38] However, there appears to be little reflection of this principle within the design of the social protection system with most benefits distributed on the basis of categorical considerations (e.g., retired, disabled) rather than on an assessment of underlying need. Moreover, Azerbaijan's 0.84% of GDP spent on social assistance[39] programs is one of the lowest in the region.[40] While this may reduce the state's contingent liabilities at the time of a disaster event, it may also make it more difficult for vulnerable people to cope following a disaster event.

Summary

In comparison with many other countries in the CAREC region, Azerbaijan is in a relatively robust financial position to respond to the financial implications of disaster events. Its disaster response funds are relatively well capitalized, and these are supported by a robust macroeconomic context and a small but growing property insurance market. In particular, whereas many other countries in the CAREC region would struggle to meet the emergency response costs associated with all but the most frequent events, Azerbaijan's reserve funds seem well placed to meet these costs for all but the most severe events.

However, there are still gaps within its disaster risk financing strategy that could be explored further. As is appropriate under a risk layering strategy, the current reserve funds (risk retention) mechanisms are insufficient to meet the direct losses of more severe events, but there are no other ex ante mechanisms in place. While the country might be able to rely on it strong fiscal position created by hydrocarbon exports to rely on borrowing to meet these losses in the short term, this may be less viable as global decarbonization efforts gather pace. It may also be valuable to consider whether the country's social protection mechanisms are designed to support recovery from disaster events, which may be particularly important in the Aran region where risks are high, but development indicators relatively lag.

---

[38]   ADB. *Azerbaijan 2020: Look into the Future, Concept of Development.* https://www.adb.org/sites/default/files/linked-documents/cps-aze-2014-2018-sd-06.pdf.

[39]   Social assistance includes cash transfers, noncontributory pensions, food and in-kind transfers, school feeding, public works schemes, fee waivers and health subsidies, and other social assistance such as scholarships and social care. Contributory pensions and government-provided health insurance are not included.

[40]   World Bank Data. Azerbaijan. https://www.worldbank.org/en/data/datatopics/aspire/country/azerbaijan (accessed May 2021).

Georgia

Flood and Earthquake Risk

Flood risk is particularly important in Georgia. Most of the losses caused by floods comes from high frequency, low severity events and, in total, floods are associated with an average AAL of around $32 million (rising to $38 million when indirect losses are included). By contrast, earthquakes happen less frequently and the AAL is somewhat lower at $14 million (rising to $18 million with indirect losses). The combined AAL as a percentage of GNI is 0.08%, one of the lowest in the CAREC region, with just Mongolia having a lower percentage.[41] Figure 11 provides the associated exceedance probability curves.

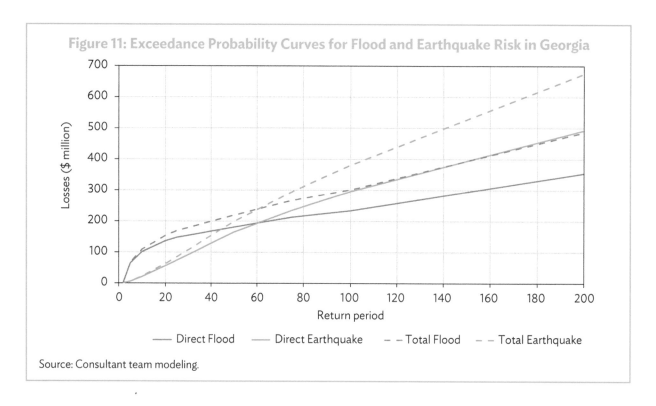

Figure 11: Exceedance Probability Curves for Flood and Earthquake Risk in Georgia

Source: Consultant team modeling.

Floods, in particular, are expected to cause significant human losses in Georgia. On average, it is estimated that floods will cause 165 deaths in Georgia each year, the sixth-highest absolute mortality associated with floods across the CAREC region. On average, 9,494 will be severely affected by floods each year. For earthquakes, the expected mortality is lower at just 11 deaths, and the number of people expected to be severely affected by earthquakes at 2,857.

Within the country, as shown in Figure 12, absolute direct losses are expected to be highest in Tbilisi, consistent with the largest concentration of economic activity and exposure in the capital. However, Kvemo Kartli province is expected to see the second-largest total amount of losses and the largest number of deaths (in both cases, driven particularly by flood events). It is also a province where development challenges are more pronounced than elsewhere in Georgia with a Human Development Index score of 0.736, the second lowest of all provinces in Georgia for which data is available. SMEs accounted for 55% of employment in Kvemo Kartli in 2016, with industry and manufacturing in particular being more important to the region than it is in other parts of the country.[42]

---

[41]   XUAR percentage is as a percentage of regional GDP rather than GNI.

[42]   Ministry of Regional Development and Infrastructure of Georgia and the European Union (undated). *Regional Development Programme of Georgia 2018–2021.* http://extwprlegs1.fao.org/docs/pdf/geo185566ENG.pdf.

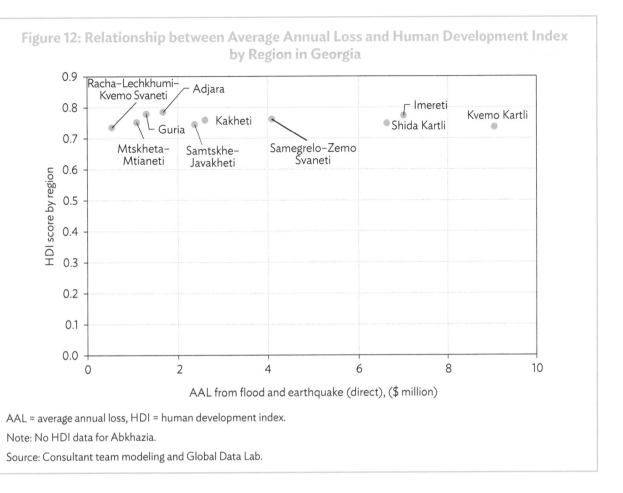

Figure 12: Relationship between Average Annual Loss and Human Development Index by Region in Georgia

AAL = average annual loss, HDI = human development index.

Note: No HDI data for Abkhazia.

Source: Consultant team modeling and Global Data Lab.

Risk Retention and Insurance Penetration

While Georgia does not currently have an explicit strategy or policy in place for managing the financial impact of disaster events, it does have a range of different financial options that it can draw upon. Municipalities (as well as the two autonomous regions of Georgia) can allocate up to 2% of the annual budget allocation into a reserve fund. These funds are not exclusively earmarked for disaster events but rather can be used for all unforeseen expenditures, with allocation decisions made by mayors or municipal governors. In 2016, the total amount of reserve funds in municipalities was GEL15 million (about $6.3 million).[43]

If these are exhausted, national level financing arrangements can be drawn upon. One of the most important of these is the Ministry of Finance "Fund for Projects Implemented in the Regions of Georgia" (RegFund), which has three spending areas, one of which is related to disaster response. In 2019, GEL410 million ($132 million) was allocated to this fund, and in 2020, GEL350 million ($113 million).[44] The role of this fund can be seen following the Tbilisi floods of 2015 when GEL71.1 million ($30 million) was allocated to disaster response.[45]

[43]   World Bank. 2017. *Disaster Risk Finance Note: Georgia.* http://documents1.worldbank.org/curated/en/929561510329276686/pdf/121242-WP-P155421-PUBLIC-32p-DRFIGeorgiaDiagnosticWeb.pdf.

[44]   Ministry of Finance of Georgia. 2020. *Citizen's Guide: Law on State Budget.* https://mof.ge/images/File/guides/Citizens%20Guide%20-%20 2020%20kanoni%20ENG%20LAST-04.pdf.

[45]   World Bank. 2017. *Disaster Risk Finance Note: Georgia.* http://documents1.worldbank.org/curated/en/929561510329276686/pdf/121242-WP-P155421-PUBLIC-32p-DRFIGeorgiaDiagnosticWeb.pdf.

In addition, the Reserve Fund of the Government and the Reserve Fund of the President can support disaster response. In both cases, a maximum of 2% of the annual budget allocation can be allocated to each fund. In 2020, GEL5 million ($1.6 million) was allocated to the Reserve Fund of the President and GEL50 million ($16.2 million) was allocated to the Reserve Fund of the Government (footnote 43). Resources from these two funds are used for expenditures not already included in the budget. The Budget Code of Georgia specifies that they are for contingencies of national significance such as disasters triggered by natural hazards and human-induced disasters. Decisions on use of these reserve funds are taken by the president (for disasters triggered by natural hazards) and the government (for human-induced disasters), in accordance with the amounts provided for in the national budget and executed by the Ministry of Finance. However, even in years where there have been significant disaster events in Georgia, such as in 2015 with the Tbilisi floods, only a relatively small proportion of the budgeted resources for these funds were used for disaster response (only 4% of the president's funds, and 2.9% of the government's funds) (footnote 44).

There is a procedure in place to allow for budget reallocations to complement these reserve funds. With the approval of the Minister of Finance, each ministry has the right to reallocate a set amount—up to 5% of the allotments envisaged by the annual budget for the ministry—from one budget line to another. A municipality may, within its powers, use its own receipts at its discretion. According to the National Progress Report on the Implementation of the Hyogo Framework for Action, reallocations are one of the primary sources of finance for high-impact disasters in Georgia.[46]

Georgia's nonlife insurance penetration rate is 1.1%, the third highest in the region. Health, property, and motor insurance compose the majority of premium payments, of which property insurance represents roughly 16% of the market.[47] The nonlife penetration rate of 1.1% and insurance density of $50 is the highest in the region with the exception of the autonomous regions of the People's Republic of China (PRC) (footnote 30). Earthquake insurance is concentrated in Tbilisi. Earthquake insurance is either included as standard with property insurance, or may be offered as an add-on, but is not offered as a stand-alone policy. Market reports suggest that around 5% of domestic properties in Tbilisi are insured, and it is likely that earthquake insurance is equally broad in its coverage. Outside of Tbilisi, very little property or earthquake cover exists.[48]

Flood insurance is offered as an extension to property insurance, but coverage is limited. Insured losses only covered 5% of the $86 million loss caused in the 2015 landslides and flooding in the Tbilisi region (footnote 47). Efforts at extending insurance cover to the agriculture sector have not been particularly successful. Perils covered by typical agriculture insurance products include hail, flood, storm, and autumn frost, with the government providing subsidies amounting to 70% of premiums. However, in 2018 only 7,800 policies were purchased, with purchases concentrated in Kakheti and for citrus fruits. In 2015, it is estimated that only 3.6% of the potentially insurable agricultural land benefited from insurance. The low take-up of agricultural insurance is reported to reflect the requirement for land to be registered before an insurance policy can be written, limited awareness, the relatively small number of sales agents and a lack of agrometeorological data leading to high premiums.[49]

[46]   Ministry of Environment and Natural Resources Protection of Georgia. 2015. *National Progress Report on the Implementation of the Hyogo Framework for Action.* https://www.preventionweb.net/files/43006_GEO_NationalHFAprogress_2013-15.pdf.

[47]   xPrimm. Georgia. https://www.xprimm.com/Georgia-2,12,47.htm.

[48]   Market reports provided by Willis Towers Watson.

[49]   I. Katsia and S. Deisadze. 2019. How can you be sure? On Georgian Agricultural Insurance. *Georgia Today.* 24 June. http://gtarchive.georgiatoday.ge/news/16191/How-Can-You-Be-Sure?-On-Georgian-Agricultural-Insurance-#:~:text=In%202014%2C%20the%20Government%20of,investment%2C%20and%20increase%20agricultural%20production.

Quantification of the Protection Gap

Average annual losses from flood and earthquake combined are estimated at $46 million. This would increase to $56 million including indirect losses but these are excluded from the base-case analysis as most of these losses will be borne by individuals and households.

Property insurance premiums, as a percentage of AAL associated with these hazards, are higher than in any other country in the CAREC region. The analysis therefore assumes that 12% of the losses associated with either peril in Tbilisi might be covered by insurance. This is higher than the 5% of losses following the Tbilisi floods of 2015 but allows for growth in the insurance market in the last 6 years. It also takes account of market reports that indicate that 5% of residential properties in Tbilisi benefit from insurance against these perils and allows for nonresidential property insurance to be higher (although payouts may be lower than total losses). Outside Tbilisi, the analysis assumes that insurance penetration rates are 50% lower, i.e., 6% of losses might be covered by insurance.

The analysis also takes account of the various risk retention funds that the government has available. It is assumed that the full capitalization of the municipality, Reserve Fund of the President and Reserve Funds of the Government could be made available following a disaster event. Recognizing that the purpose of the RegFund is not just to provide contingency funding, it is assumed that $30 million could be made available, equal to the amount made available from this Fund after the 2015 Tbilisi floods.

The results of the analysis are presented in Figure 13 and Table 6. Compared to other countries in the CAREC region, a greater proportion of the finanial risks associated with disaster events are covered by existing measures. With the stated assumptions, all the AAL associated with floods and earthquakes could be covered.

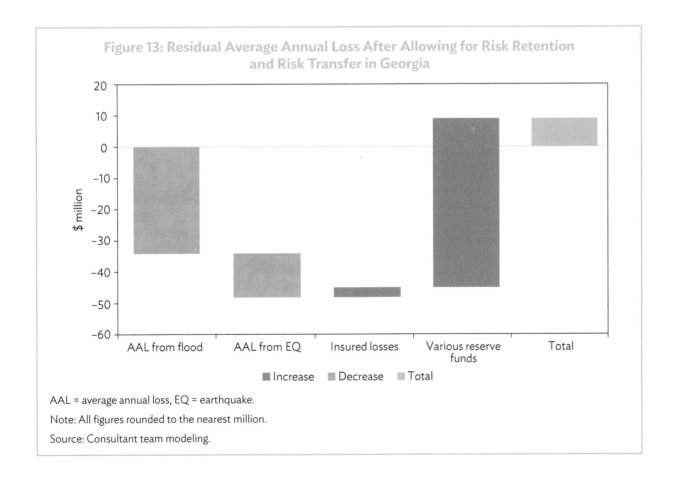

Figure 13: Residual Average Annual Loss After Allowing for Risk Retention and Risk Transfer in Georgia

AAL = average annual loss, EQ = earthquake.

Note: All figures rounded to the nearest million.

Source: Consultant team modeling.

However, looking at the possibility of more extreme events, if the existing mechanisms were expected to cover all uninsured direct losses, then they would be exhausted by a 1 in 5-year flood event or by a 1 in 25-year earthquake event. In the case of floods, the same threshold applies if these measures also needed to cover the indirect losses associated with events as well. For earthquakes, however, only a 1 in 20-year event could be covered in the case where indirect losses must also be covered. If the risk retention mechanisms are only intended to be used in relation to emergency response costs, then they would be exhausted by a 1 in 200-year flood or earthquake event.

Table 6: Event Frequeny at which Ex Ante Mechanisms Are Exhausted in Georgia

Event frequency where direct and indirect losses, less (assumed) insured losses, exceed existing ex ante risk retention		Event frequency where direct losses, less (assumed) insured losses, exceed existing ex ante risk retention		Event frequency where estimated emergency response costs exceed current risk retention mechanisms	
Flood	**Earthquake**	**Flood**	**Earthquake**	**Flood**	**Earthquake**
1 in 5	1 in 20	1 in 5	1 in 25	1 in 200	1 in 200

Source: Consultant team modeling.

Ability to Rely on Ex Post Borrowing

Georgia's fiscal position had been strengthening prior to the impact of the COVID-19 crisis. In October 2019, Standard & Poor's upgraded Georgia's credit rating, although still considered non-investment grade, citing strong growth prospects and prudent public financial management.[50] The IMF had also assessed the public debt position to be sustainable over the medium term.[51] However, COVID-19 has at least temporarily weakened government finances, with 2020 seeing a spike in public debt and the fiscal deficit widening to 9.3% of GDP. Its fiscal position is also made more vulnerable because of 75% of its public debt being denominated in foreign currency, coupled with the central bank having low foreign exchange reserves.[52] This makes the country vulnerable to exchange rate shocks. Nonetheless, the country's credit rating remains higher than that of many other CAREC countries and the government debt position is expected to decline into the medium term. Figure 14 summarizes.

Georgian individuals and households are also more likely to be able to access finance to help respond to disaster events than those in other countries in the CAREC region. Bank account ownership stands above 60%, and a higher proportion of women than men own an account (footnote 24). Social protection spending by the government is also large by regional standards, with Georgia spending 6.59% of GDP on social assistance in 2013, the next largest spender on social assistance in the region is the Kyrgyz Republic at 2.6%. In total, 64% of the population is covered by social insurance, social safety nets and unemployment benefit programming, rising to 71% of the bottom income quintile. In 2012, the government launched the targeted social assistance program, a means-tested social program that identifies the most vulnerable families to provide targeted support. As a consequence, 44% of all social assistance spent goes to the poorest 20% of the population.[53] However, while such programs are likely to support Georgia in being able to respond to disaster events, they do also imply an increased contingent liability on the government's finances.

There are also likely to be important differences in the financial resilience of different subgroups within Georgia. For instance, compared to the 61% bank account ownership for the population as a whole, only 31% of young adults

[50] D. Istrate. 2019. *S&P upgrades Georgia's credit ratings.* Emerging Europe. 15 October. https://emerging-europe.com/news/sp-upgrades-georgias-credit-ratings/.

[51] IMF. 2020. *Georgia: Sixth Review Under the Extended Arrangement and Requests for a Waiver of Nonobservance of Performance Criterion, Modification of Performance Criteria, and Augmentation of Access.* https://www.imf.org/en/Publications/CR/Issues/2020/05/05/Georgia-Sixth-Review-Under-the-Extended-Arrangement-and-Requests-for-a-Waiver-of-49394.

[52] World Bank. 2022. *Data: Total Reserves in Months of Imports – Georgia.* https://data.worldbank.org/indicator/FI.RES.TOTL.MO?locations=GE.

[53] *Global Partnership for Financial Inclusion.* https://datatopics.worldbank.org/g20fidata/country/georgia.

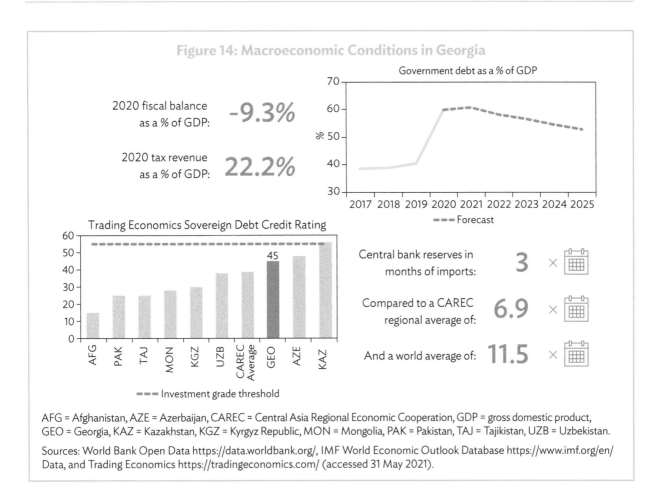

Figure 14: Macroeconomic Conditions in Georgia

2020 fiscal balance as a % of GDP: **-9.3%**

2020 tax revenue as a % of GDP: **22.2%**

Government debt as a % of GDP

Trading Economics Sovereign Debt Credit Rating

Central bank reserves in months of imports: **3** × 🗓

Compared to a CAREC regional average of: **6.9** × 🗓

And a world average of: **11.5** × 🗓

--- Investment grade threshold

AFG = Afghanistan, AZE = Azerbaijan, CAREC = Central Asia Regional Economic Cooperation, GDP = gross domestic product, GEO = Georgia, KAZ = Kazakhstan, KGZ = Kyrgyz Republic, MON = Mongolia, PAK = Pakistan, TAJ = Tajikistan, UZB = Uzbekistan.

Sources: World Bank Open Data https://data.worldbank.org/, IMF World Economic Outlook Database https://www.imf.org/en/Data, and Trading Economics https://tradingeconomics.com/ (accessed 31 May 2021).

(aged 15–24) own an account (footnote 24). This likely reflects the low rates of economic activity among this group. Georgia has a youth unemployment rate of around 28% compared to the national average of 17.6%.[54] There are also differences in financial inclusion and financial literacy between urban and rural areas although these are less stark than in other CAREC countries (55% of the rural population own a bank account compared to 61% for the population as a whole).

Summary

Georgia and its citizens are in a stronger place to manage the financial impacts of disaster events than many other countries in the CAREC region. Its reserve funds are currently large enough to cope with the average annual losses that might arise from these events, or to cover the emergency response costs associated with a 1 in 200-year flood or earthquake. This is buttressed by a relatively benign macroeconomic context (relative to some other countries in the CAREC region) and levels of financial inclusion and social assistance that will provide resilience, at least to high frequency, low severity events.

However, there are obvious gaps. Most notably, the current risk retention mechanisms would be exhausted by the direct losses caused by floods with a return period of 1 in 5 years. While the costs of retaining reserves for more severe events may be prohibitively high, it does create a potential financing gap, especially outside of Tbilisi where the penetration of private insurance markets remains weak. The province of Kvemo Kartli may be of particular concern given its high flood risk coupled with, by the standards elsewhere in the country, its relatively low HDI ranking.

---

[54] National Statistics Office of Georgia. *Employment and Unemployment.* https://www.geostat.ge/en/modules/categories/683/Employment-Unemployment (accessed May 2021).

Kazakhstan

Flood and Earthquake Risk

Flood risk is much more pronounced than earthquake risk in Kazakhstan (Figure 15). The AAL for floods is estimated to be $419 million, more than seven times higher than for earthquake risk ($58 million). Including indirect losses, the AALs for floods and earthquakes increase to $447 million and $73 million respectively. The exceedance probability curves show that the losses caused by floods rises sharply over events up to a 1 in 25-year return period, with rarer events causing only moderately more loss. The combined AAL as a proportion of GNI excluding indirect losses is 0.11%, which is the eighth highest of all countries and provinces in the region.

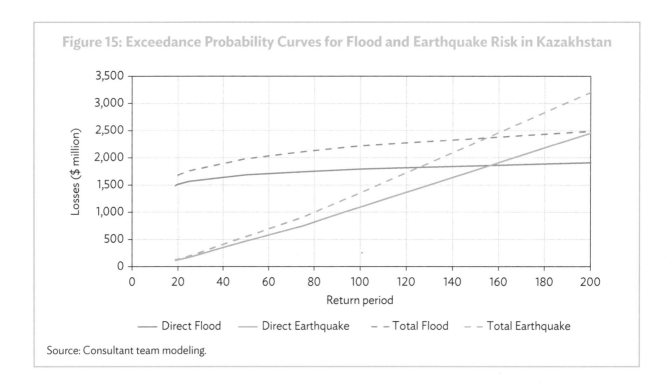

Figure 15: Exceedance Probability Curves for Flood and Earthquake Risk in Kazakhstan

Source: Consultant team modeling.

The significance of flood risk in Kazakhstan is further reinforced by the estimates of average annual loss of life. At 392 deaths per year, this is around 66% higher than any other country in the CAREC region. In addition, more than 61,000 people, on average, are expected to be severely affected by flooding each year. Earthquakes are expected to be responsible for an average 42 deaths per year, in the middle of the range for CAREC countries, with almost 6,500 expected to be severely affected by earthquakes.

Within the country, the two regions that combine both high AALs from flood and earthquake and, comparatively, high proportions of people living in multidimensional poverty are Turkestan and Kyzylorda (Figure 16). In both cases, flood is the predominant peril in terms of AAL. However, the proportion of people living in multidimensional poverty in any region in Kazakhstan is substantially lower than in most other countries for which data is available.

Economic activity in Kyzylorda is heavily dominated by fossil fuel extraction. In Turkestan, economic activity, as measured by exports, is dominated by refined fuels (65%) and agribusiness (10%) with smaller amounts of exports in basic chemicals and fertilizers but little export activity in final consumer products. Agricultural production is also important in Turkestan. A 2015 report states that there were 126,000 SMEs in Turkestan, the highest number among all regions in the country.[55]

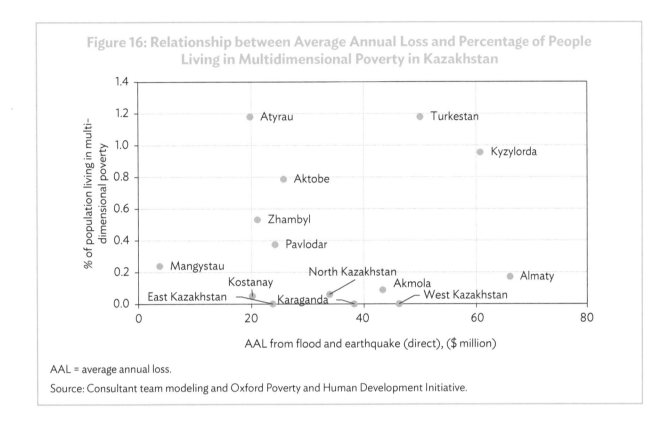

Figure 16: Relationship between Average Annual Loss and Percentage of People Living in Multidimensional Poverty in Kazakhstan

AAL = average annual loss.

Source: Consultant team modeling and Oxford Poverty and Human Development Initiative.

Risk Retention and Insurance Penetration

Kazakhstan has a number of reserve funds and contingency arrangements for dealing with the financial consequences of disaster events. According to the Law on Civil Protection, compensation for harm and damages is first the responsibility of local government, which are expected to develop reserve funds with allocations capped at 2% of budgetary revenues. There is also a national reserve fund for supporting livelihoods after a human-induced disaster, or disaster triggered by natural hazards. In 2021, the allocation for this fund was around $804 million.[56] Annual allocation to the reserve fund is capped at 2% of the total annual budget. In addition, there is also a contingency reserve, established by the provision of the Committee of Emergency Situations, to cover disaster response and recovery costs such as medical assistance and rescue operations. The total allocation for these costs in 2021 was around $39 million.[57]

55   Whiteshield Partners. 2015. *Diversification of Kazakhstan's Economy: A Capability-Based Approach.* https://www.ebrd.com/documents/comms-and-bis/diversification-of-kazakhstans-economy.pdf.

56   Under Article 19 of the budget, the budget for the reserve fund was set at T343,744,844,000. https://online.zakon.kz/m/Document/?doc_id=32245090. Converted to United States (US) dollars using an exchange rate of 1:0.0023.

57   Under Article 20 of the budget, funds for the formation and storage of the formation and storage of the state material reserve in the amount of T12,917,877,000 with a further T3,585,654,000 available from the sale of tangible assets. https://online.zakon.kz/m/Document/?doc_id=32245090. Converted to US dollars using an exchange rate of 1:0.0023.

In all cases, allocations are made annually and cannot be carried forward. If these resources are exhusted, the government expects to reallocate and borrow. As a matter of course, government budget allocations can be changed once per year, as well as additionally in emergency situations. At a 2019 forum hosted by the World Bank, representatives from the government stated that from their perspective, an important first step before developing any further risk finance instruments would be to understand what financing instruments are appropriate for the country and only then elaborate on appropriate measures for financial preparedness against natural hazards.[58]

The nonlife insurance penetration rate in Kazakhstan is around 0.5%, placing the country in the middle third of CAREC region countries. Of this, around one quarter nonlife insurance premiums are attributed to property insurance, which includes earthquake, flooding, and fire coverage.[59] At the same forum referred to above, it was discussed that the government had been exploring the possibility of introducing mandatory disaster insurance for private property, although no official government announcement has been made (footnote 57).

Until 2020, crop insurance was compulsory, but this has recently changed. The compulsory nature of the policy meant that 75% of the eligible crop area was covered. However, the policy was costly for insurers to administer, the meteorological reports were often delayed or inaccurate, and insurer payouts only covered an average of 20% of the farmers' losses.[60] From 2020, compulsory crop insurance has been replaced with a voluntary index-based insurance for crops and animal husbandry.

Quantifying the Protection Gap

Total direct AAL from flood and earthquake events sums to around $477 million per year. Indirect losses increase this to over $520 million, but the indirect losses are excluded from the base-case analysis.

There is little data available on the proportion of property exposures benefiting from insurance. However, property insurance premiums as a percentage of AALs from flood and earthquake events are among the highest in the CAREC region (61%). Calibrating this datapoint against other countries where more information on insurance penetration is available suggests that an assumption that around 7% of AAL might be insured is reasonable.[61] In addition, it is assumed that the full amount of the national reserve fund an the contingency reserve ($843 million) is available to support the response from disasters.

This leads to the conclusion that the combination of insurance and retention instruments is sufficient to cover the expected annual loss from the combination of flood and earthquake events, as shown in Figure 17. Looking at the impact of more extreme events in Table 7, current financing arrangements might be exhausted by an earthquake event of 1 in 100 years (or 1 in 75 when considering indirect losses). For floods, a 1 in 10-year event might cause the exhaustion of existing financing mechanisms if all losses were to be met by these arrangements. If these financing mechanisms are intended to only cover emergency response costs, then they are sufficient to cover these costs for earthquake or flood events with a return period of over 1 in 200-years.

[58]   World Bank. 2019. *Forum on Financial Protection against Natural Disasters in Central Asia.* Almaty, Kazakhstan. 26–27 February.
[59]   RAExpert. 2019. *Central Asia Industry Research – Insurance.* https://raexpert.eu/files/Industry_report_Insurance_CA_01.11.2019.pdf.
[60]   World Bank. 2012. *Kazakhstan: Agricultural Insurance Feasibility Study.* https://documents1.worldbank.org/curated/en/983671468041118238/pdf/9 22300v10WP0Ka010Box385354B00OUO090.pdf.
[61]   For example, in the Georgia analysis, property insurance premiums as a percent of flood and earthquake AAL is calculated as 61% and in this case it is estimated that around 7.2% of AAL might be covered by insurance.

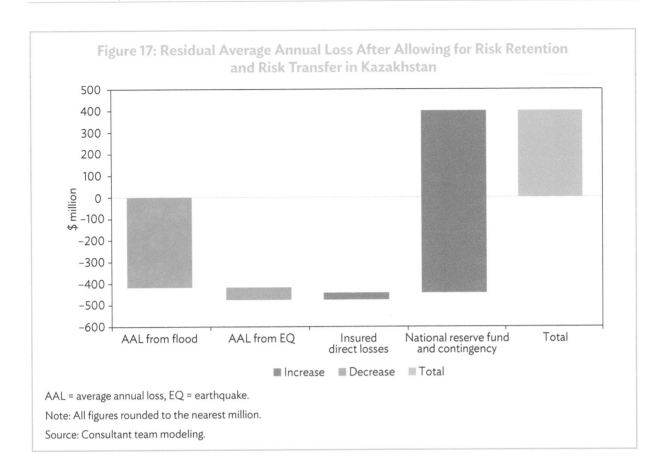

Figure 17: Residual Average Annual Loss After Allowing for Risk Retention and Risk Transfer in Kazakhstan

AAL = average annual loss, EQ = earthquake.

Note: All figures rounded to the nearest million.

Source: Consultant team modeling.

Table 7: Event Frequency at which Ex Ante Mechanisms Are Exhausted in Kazakhstan

Event frequency where direct and indirect losses, less (assumed) insured losses, exceed existing ex ante risk retention		Event frequency where direct losses, less (assumed) insured losses, exceed existing ex ante risk retention		Event frequency where estimated emergency response costs exceed current risk retention mechanisms	
Flood	**Earthquake**	**Flood**	**Earthquake**	**Flood**	**Earthquake**
1 in 10	1 in 75	1 in 10	1 in 100	>1 in 200	>1 in 200

Source: Consultant team modeling.

Ability to Rely on Ex Post Borrowing

The fiscal position of Kazakhstan is robust, although the COVID-19 crisis has demonstrated some weaknesses. Public debt is low by the standards of the CAREC region although it is expected to remain persistently higher than it was before the COVID-19 crisis.[62] Kazakhstan is the only country in the CAREC region (except for the PRC) that enjoys an investment grade rating on its sovereign debt. However, much of the country's debt is short-term. In 2019, total debts maturing were equivalent to 5.8% of GDP (footnote 61). This means that the impact of changes in fiscal health arising from changes in the external environment quickly feed through into budgetary impact. This is important in a context in which the yield on 10-year bonds issued in tenge have increased by about 10% since the beginning of March 2020.[63]

[62]   World Bank. 2021. *A Cross-Country Database of Fiscal Space.* https://www.worldbank.org/en/research/brief/fiscal-space.
[63]   Organisation for Economic Co-operation and Development. 2020. *The COVID-19 Crisis in Kazakhstan.* https://www.oecd.org/eurasia/competitiveness-programme/central-asia/Covid-19-CRISIS-IN-KAZAKHSTAN.pdf.

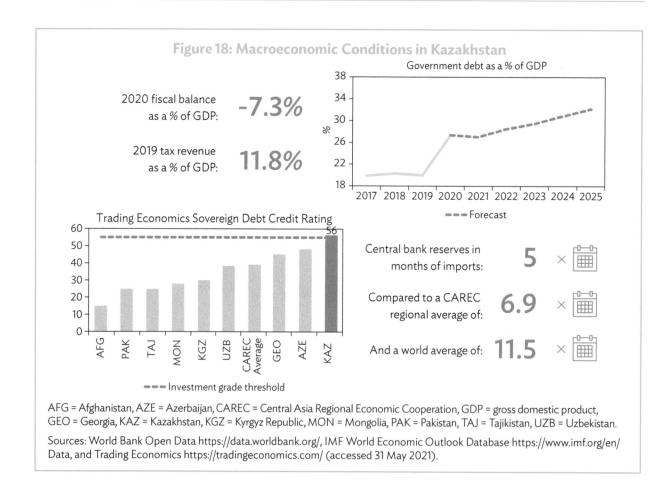

Figure 18: Macroeconomic Conditions in Kazakhstan

AFG = Afghanistan, AZE = Azerbaijan, CAREC = Central Asia Regional Economic Cooperation, GDP = gross domestic product, GEO = Georgia, KAZ = Kazakhstan, KGZ = Kyrgyz Republic, MON = Mongolia, PAK = Pakistan, TAJ = Tajikistan, UZB = Uzbekistan.

Sources: World Bank Open Data https://data.worldbank.org/, IMF World Economic Outlook Database https://www.imf.org/en/Data, and Trading Economics https://tradingeconomics.com/ (accessed 31 May 2021).

Notwithstanding the bond yield increase, the COVID-19 crisis has broadly demonstrated the underlying fiscal health of the country, relative to other countries in the CAREC region. The government has been able to provide a large economic response package—equivalent to around 15% of GDP—largely through the finances associated with its oil reserves. This is much greater than the regional average of 8.0% of GDP. Support from international financial institutions has been less than 5% of this amount.

Considering households and individuals, financial inclusion, and hence likely ability to access finance after a disaster event is also relatively good in comparison to other countries in the CAREC region. Fifty-nine percent of the adult population own a bank account and 14% have saved at a financial institution. There is very little difference in these figures between men and women or between urban and rural populations (footnote 24).

However, poorer members of society may be disproportionately vulnerable. Bank account ownership for the poorest two quintiles of the population is significantly lower than the rest of the population, as is the saving rate, with only 7.5% of the poorest two quintiles of population saving at a financial institution, compared to 14% of the total population (footnote 24). These challenges may be exacerbated by a social protection system that is not particularly well-targeted at low-income households: research suggests that poor households that do not have two or more children or a household member with a disability often do not receive the minimum income needed to address their basic needs, even though they are eligible based on their household income.[64] Consistent with this, 41% of the poorest quintile of households in Kazakhstan are not covered by social policy or labor market programs.[65]

---

[64]   J. Hagen-Zanker and H. Salomon. 2015. *Analysis of Social Transfers for Children and their Families in Kazakhstan.* UNICEF. https://socialprotection.org/discover/publications/analysis-social-transfers-children-and-their-families-kazakhstan.
[65]   World Bank ASPIRE Database. https://www.worldbank.org/en/data/datatopics/aspire (accessed May 2021).

Summary

Kazakhstan faces significant flood risk, especially when measured in terms of expected lives lost. Moreover, a significant proportion of this risk is concentrated in regions of the country that are already suffering from comparatively high levels of poverty (Turkestan and Kyzylorda). However, the state has reasonably significant financial resources through its existing risk retention mechanisms. These are estimated to be sufficient, at least, to be able to cover the AALs expected from floods and earthquakes. However, there may be value in considering risk transfer mechanisms associated with more extreme (flood) events in particular, though given the investment grade credit rating of the country, the cost efficiency of such mechanisms compared to ex post borrowing would need to be assessed carefully. Given the concentration of flood risk in areas of the country where poverty is more pronounced, there may be value in exploring opportunities for boosting the financial inclusion and targeting of social protection toward these vulnerable populations.

Kyrgyz Republic

Flood and Earthquake Risk

The Kyrgyz Republic faces substantial risks from both earthquake and floods. The AAL associated with flood is more than $73 million and that associated with earthquake is $72 million yielding an aggregate AAL of nearly $146 million[66] ($89 million, $102 million and $191 million when including indirect losses). The direct AAL is equivalent to 0.44% of GNI, the highest proportion of any country in the CAREC region. As Figure 19 shows, and following a common pattern, high frequency, low severity flood events dominate the flood risk profile, whereas earthquake risk is driven by lower frequency, higher severity events.

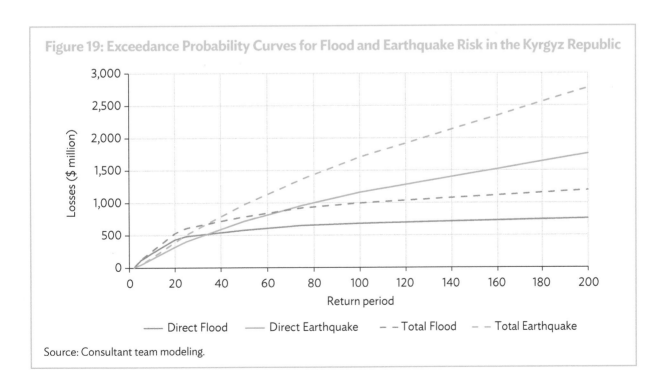

Figure 19: Exceedance Probability Curves for Flood and Earthquake Risk in the Kyrgyz Republic

Source: Consultant team modeling.

---

[66] The figures in the text do not sum due to rounding.

These events are also associated with significant human losses. Flood events, in particular, are expected to be associated with 193 deaths per year on average, the fourth-highest number of any country. Earthquakes are expected to cause 27 deaths per year on average. However, when looked at the from the perspective of the number of people expected to be severely affected by the two perils, the relative importance reverses: just over 4,400 people are expected to be severely affected by floods, rising to 5,570 for people expected to be severely affected by earthquakes.

There are few people living in multidimensional poverty in the Kyrgyz Republic and most of those that do meet this criteria are not living in the highest risk areas. In particular, the two highest risk regions by AAL—Osh City and Chui have relatively small proportions of people living in multidimensional poverty. Chui is also the province expected to see the largest loss of life from floods and earthquakes. The two regions of greatest concern from the combination of poverty and risk are Osh[67] and Jalal–Abad, as shown in Figure 20. In both regions, there is significant agricultural (and some agro-processing) activity: in Osh, SMEs are particularly evident in the potato production and apple value chains; in Jalal–Abad apples, apricots and plums are important products for SMEs.[68] In Jalal–Abad this is complemented by a number of medium-sized enterprises in the industrial sector including in textile and leather manufacturing, construction, and confectionery. There are also larger firms in the energy and mining sector in Jalal–Abad.[69]

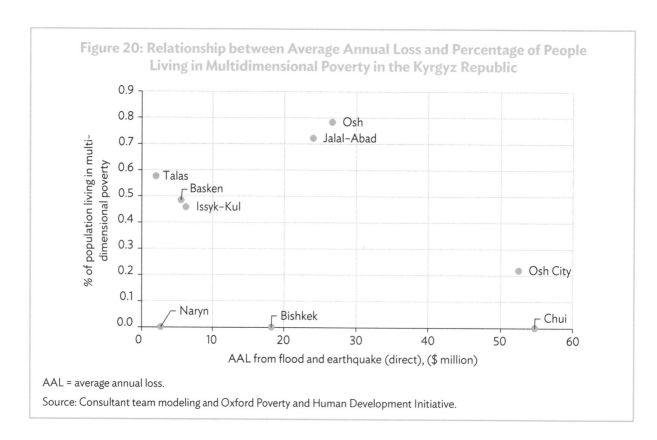

Figure 20: Relationship between Average Annual Loss and Percentage of People Living in Multidimensional Poverty in the Kyrgyz Republic

AAL = average annual loss.

Source: Consultant team modeling and Oxford Poverty and Human Development Initiative.

[67]   Noting that Osh and Osh City are different provinces.

[68]   International Labour Organization. 2018. *Assessment of Select Horticultural Sectors in Kyrgyzstan, and their Market Access Potential.* https://www.ilo.org/wcmsp5/groups/public/---ed_emp/---emp_ent/documents/publication/wcms_652326.pdf.

[69]   N. Komendantova, N. Atakanov, U. Chekirbaev, N. Karabashov, Z. Zheenaliev, E. Rovsenskaya, N. Strelkovskii, S. Sizov, and F. Santiago-Rodriguez. 2018. *Industrial Development of Kyrgyzstan: Regional Aspects.* https://www.unido.org/sites/default/files/files/2018-12/Industrial_Development_Kyrgyzstan-Regional_aspects.pdf.

Risk Retention and Insurance Penetration

Disaster response in the Kyrgyz Republic is initially funded by the budgets of the Ministry of Emergency Situations and the local governments. If these resources are exhausted, then additional funds can be requested from the Ministry of Finance that can make use of emergency accounts, as established by Resolution 509 of the Government of the Kyrgyz Republic 2007, and state budget reserves and from reallocation of the budget or other sources. In total, it is estimated that there is around $60 million in reserve funds available to support disaster response. However, this funding is not earmarked specifically for disasters (footnote 57).

Disaster recovery and reconstruction is financed through the relevant budget lines of line ministries or local governments or through a request to the Ministry of Finance. The Ministry of Finance responds to these requests on a case-by-case basis. Typical sources of finance for such requests include budget reallocation or borrowing (including from development partners), from donor aid, or by approval of additional dedicated budget allocations for disaster response and rehabilitation in the annual national budget. There are no sovereign focused risk transfer arrangements. However, at a 2019 Forum, the Kyrgyz Republic identified an interest in risk pools and supported efforts to consolidate regional efforts on disaster risk financing (footnote 57).

For the countries for which data is available, the Kyrgyz Republic has the smallest retail nonlife insurance market in the region, both in terms of penetration and density. The penetration rate for insurance products is just 0.2% (footnote 30). Of this, 12.5% is estimated to be property insurance (footnote 58). This is despite disaster insurance for houses—usually including earthquake and flood protection—being mandatory since 2015 with coverage provided by the State Insurance Company. However, it is estimated that only between 6.5%[70] and 9% (footnote 57) of the housing stock are covered, due to unaffordability of the insurance premiums and wide lack of trust in the insurance industry. Mandatory coverage is set at $14,500 in urban areas and $7,250 rural areas. Market reports indicate that the limited property insurance cover is heavily concentrated in Bishkek and Osh, with efforts by the central government to push sales of property insurance in rural areas meeting with little success to date (footnote 19). However, an ongoing project by the World Bank is trying to encourage take up of household insurance including through the introduction of a web portal of the State Insurance Company.

Agricultural insurance is not widespread, and few insurers offer such cover. No statistics are provided regarding market share. However, reports suggest there is a demand for such cover, in particular for crop losses relating to hail, but insurers are unwilling to provide cover at the premiums that farmers could afford (footnote 47).

Quantifying the Protection Gap

The AAL from flood and earthquake events is assessed to be around $146 million (rising to $191 million if indirect losses were also to be included). It is assumed that in Bishkek and Osh City, 8% of these losses might be covered by insurance, falling to 2% in the rest of the country. This is equivalent to 3.0% of total losses in the country being covered. This accounts for estimates that 6.5%-9% of the housing stock have compulsory cover, taking account of the low mandatory cover and data from Swiss Re suggesting that nonlife insurance density is lower than in other CAREC countries fo which data is available. The assumed geographic distribution of insurance cover is based on market reports. In addition, it is assumed that all of the $60 million reported in the various reserve funds in the country is available to support emergency recovery and reconstruction.

---

[70]   World Bank. 2018. Kyrgyz Republic to Scale-Up Disaster and Climate Change Resilience, with World Bank Support. *News Release*. 25 May. Washington, DC. https://www.worldbank.org/en/news/press-release/2018/05/25/kyrgyz-republic-to-scale-up-disaster-and-climate-change-resilience-with-world-bank-support.

In combination, these assumptions suggest that there is a significant unfunded AAL associated with floods and earthquakes in the Kyrgyz Republic, equal to around $81 million each year (Figure 21). Consistent with this, taking account of expected insurance cover, current risk retention funding would be exhausted by a 1 in 5-year flood or 1 in 10-year earthquake event (both with and without the inclusion of indirect losses). If the risk retention mechanisms are only expected to cover emergency response costs, then they would be exhausted by a 1 in 20-year flood event or a 1 in 25-year earthquake event (Table 8).

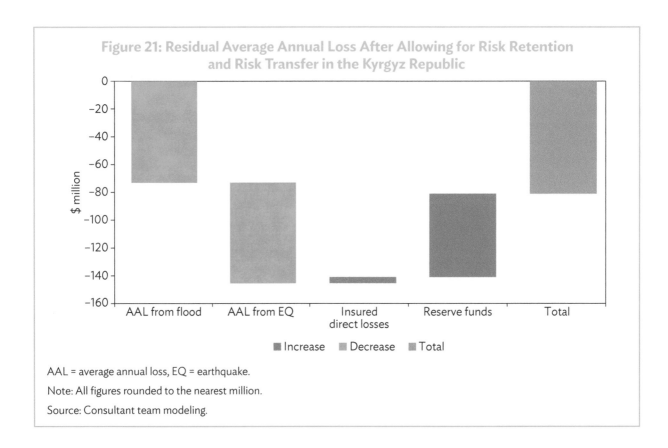

Figure 21: Residual Average Annual Loss After Allowing for Risk Retention and Risk Transfer in the Kyrgyz Republic

AAL = average annual loss, EQ = earthquake.

Note: All figures rounded to the nearest million.

Source: Consultant team modeling.

Table 8: Event Frequency at which Ex Ante Mechanisms Are Exhausted in the Kyrgyz Republic

Event frequency where direct and indirect losses, less (assumed) insured losses, exceed existing ex ante risk retention		Event frequency where direct losses, less (assumed) insured losses, exceed existing ex ante risk retention		Event frequency where estimated emergency response costs exceed current risk retention mechanisms	
Flood	Earthquake	Flood	Earthquake	Flood	Earthquake
1 in 5	1 in 10	1 in 5	1 in 10	1 in 20	1 in 25

Source: Consultant team modeling.

Ability to Rely on Ex Post Borrowing

Prior to the COVID-19 crisis, government debt was low and stable, although as it was largely denominated in foreign currency, the country remained vulnerable to an export shock or exchange rate volatility. This risk has subsequently materialized with a 20% depreciation in the value of the currency compared to the dollar since the start of the COVID-19 crisis. IMF analysis identifies that the country is at moderate risk of debt distress and identifies that the country should seek to avoid non-concessional financing to reduce its fiscal vulnerability.[71] This is consistent with a credit rating that is among the median for the CAREC region but significantly below investment grade. Figure 22 summarizes.

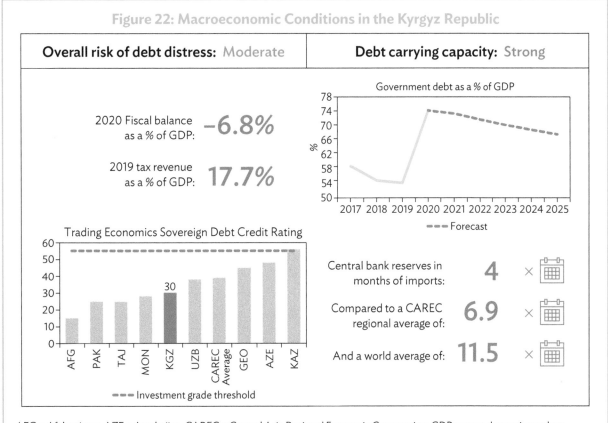

Figure 22: Macroeconomic Conditions in the Kyrgyz Republic

AFG = Afghanistan, AZE = Azerbaijan, CAREC = Central Asia Regional Economic Cooperation, GDP = gross domestic product, GEO = Georgia, KAZ = Kazakhstan, KGZ = Kyrgyz Republic, MON = Mongolia, PAK = Pakistan, TAJ = Tajikistan, UZB = Uzbekistan.

Sources: World Bank Open Data https://data.worldbank.org/, IMF World Economic Outlook Database https://www.imf.org/en/ Data, and Trading Economics https://tradingeconomics.com/ (accessed 31 May 2021).

This reflects how the country has responded to the COVID-19 crisis. The country has had to rely heavily on international support for its response—the total package of support provided is around $838 million with support from international partners amounting to $700 million. Much of the funding that has been provided has been on heavily concessional terms including $120 million in interest free loans from the IMF, $100 million from the Eurasian Fund for Stabilization and Development at a 1% interest rate, and $43 million in grants from the European Union.[72]

Financial inclusion of households is also relatively low. Account ownership is one of the lowest in the region at 40%, and only 3% of the population report having saved at a financial institution, compared to regional averages of 44.6% and 7.5% respectively (footnote 24). There are also important regional disparities with over half of loans and over 80% of deposits registered in Bishkek, the capital city.[73]

---

[71] IMF. 2020. Kyrgyz Republic. Request for Purchase under the Rapid Financing Instrument and Disbursement under the Rapid Credit Facility – Debt Sustainability Analysis. *Country Report* No. 20/90. March. Washington, DC. https://www.imf.org/en/Publications/CR/Issues/2020/03/27/ Kyrgyz-Republic-Request-for-Purchase-Under-the-Rapid-Financing-Instrument-and-Disbursement-49296.

[72] ADB COVID-19 Policy Database (accessed May 2021). https://covid19policy.adb.org/.

[73] S. Hasanova. 2018. Financial Inclusion, Financial Regulation, Financial Literacy, and Financial Education in the Kyrgyz Republic. *ADBI Working Paper Series* No. 850. https://think-asia.org/bitstream/handle/11540/8456/adbi-wp850.pdf?sequence=1.

For households, this is partly offset by a relatively generous social assistance program, which is among the most pro-poor in the region. Social assistance programs incur about 2.6% of GDP, with 64% of the bottom income quintile covered by such programs. Thirty-five percent of benefits are targeted at the poorest 20% of society, the second-highest targeting rate in the region, behind Georgia.[74] While such provisions are important in providing support to the country's vulnerable populations, it does imply that a higher proportion of the indirect losses associated with disaster events are contingent liabilities for the government.

Summary

The current risk retention and risk transfer instruments in the Kyrgyz Republic are insufficient for the disaster risk that the country faces. The AALs from flood and earthquake events constitute a higher proportion of GNI in the Kyrgyz Republic than in other country in the CAREC region. In comparison, while efforts have been made to increase insurance penetration, coverage remains low. Similarly, government reserve funds are not large enough to cover the expected emergency response costs of a 1 in 20-year flood event. If such disasters took place, the government's ability to access capital markets in a sustainable way would be limited, making it reliant on concessional funding from international partners.

Mongolia

Flood and Earthquake Risk

Flood risk is much more significant than earthquake risk in Mongolia, as displayed in Figure 23. The estimated AAL from flood risk is around $24 million ($30 million including indirect losses), compared to just $0.6 million for earthquake risk (rising to $0.8 million with indirect losses). The combined risk of around $24.6 million is equivalent to approximately 0.07% of GNI in the country, which is the lowest of all the countries and provinces in the CAREC region.

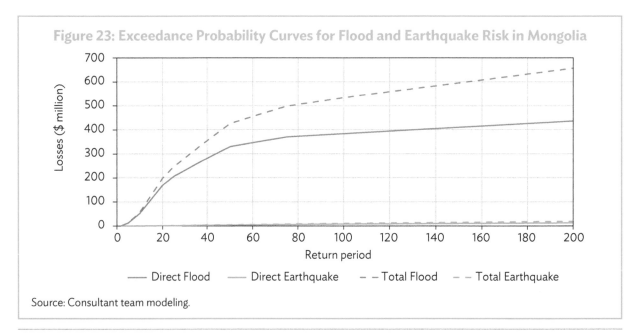

Figure 23: Exceedance Probability Curves for Flood and Earthquake Risk in Mongolia

Source: Consultant team modeling.

---

[74]   World Bank ASPIRE Database. https://www.worldbank.org/en/data/datatopics/aspire/country/kyrgyz-republic (accessed May 2021).

Unsurprisingly, the same relative pattern between flood and earthquake risk is also observed for the human losses of the two disaster events. Floods are expected to result, on average, in 92 deaths per annum in the country, whereas earthquakes are expected to be associated with 1 death, on average. Likewise, over 8,000 people are expected to be severely affected by floods in an average, but just over 100 people will be severely affected by earthquakes.

There is little overall pattern between the magnitude of flood and earthquake risk and the level of intra-regional development within the provinces. However, as shown in Figure 24, Khuvsgul may be a province of particular concern given that it is expected to suffer some of the largest losses, and it is also among the provinces with the lowest HDI scores in the country. A similar pattern emerges when considering loss of life rather than AALs. Economic activity in this province is dominated by livestock herding with herder households accounting for more than 50% of all households.[75]

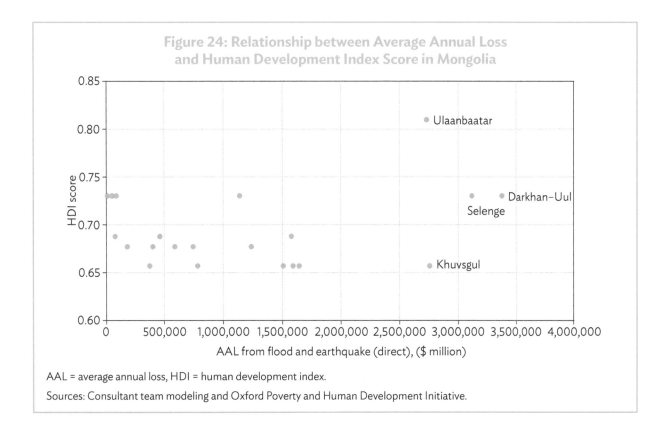

Figure 24: Relationship between Average Annual Loss and Human Development Index Score in Mongolia

AAL = average annual loss, HDI = human development index.

Sources: Consultant team modeling and Oxford Poverty and Human Development Initiative.

Risk Retention and Insurance Penetration

There are two main risk retention instruments in Mongolia:[76]

(i)   **The Government Reserve Fund.** This is used for relief expenditures due to disasters triggered by natural hazards or human-induced disasters, implementation of new legislation, government expenses in international dispute resolution, and expenditures related with international treaties. This covers the direct cost of response and recovery. The current level of funding available from this reserve is unclear,

75   D. Darbalaeva, A. Mikheeva, and Y. Zhamyanova. 2020. The Socio-Economic Consequences of the Desertification Processes in Mongolia. *E3S Web of Conferences*. 164(11001) https://doi.org/10.1051/e3sconf /202016411001.

76   World Bank. 2015. *Public Financial Management Performance Report.* https://www.adb.org/sites/default/files/linked-documents/49210-001-sd-02.pdf.

although around $26 million was spent from the Fund for disaster relief and recovery expenditure in 2013 and 2014.

(ii)   **The Contingency Fund.** This is used for unexpected large revenue shortfalls; disruption in domestic production and services including agricultural production due to unforeseeable events or disasters triggered by natural hazards; abrupt fluctuation in exchange rates; and abrupt price increases of flour, wheat, and petroleum products in domestic markets.

In addition, local governors have a Local Governors' Reserve Fund (or Disaster Protection Fund), although the combined size of these funds is unclear. Additional funding to respond to disaster events can also be made available through midyear budgetary adjustments. Importantly, these reserves also need to cover costs and losses associated with other disaster events, most notably *dzuds*.[77]

Mongolia's nonlife insurance penetration is around the median for the CAREC region at a rate of 0.6% and insurance density of $23/person.[78] Property insurance premiums account for 28% of all nonlife premiums, leading to a property insurance penetration rate of 0.17% (footnote 47). Earthquake, windstorm, and flood cover are all included in property insurance. However, market reports suggest that there have never been any notable insured losses, indicative of the low coverage rate, and the same reports suggest that there is a lack of sophisticated accumulation monitoring of exposure to these threats. Almost all property insurance is in Ulaanbaatar (footnote 47).

The agriculture sector has been supported, however, by an innovative index-based livestock insurance (IBLI) scheme. This microinsurance product, initially introduced with the support of the World Bank but provided by private insurance companies through a joint-liability pool arrangement, provides cover to herders when the district level mortality rate of a particular species exceeds a threshold of 6%. This is expected to cover losses with events of a 1 in 5-year return period. The government then provides reinsurance to all insurance companies who offer the product. The scheme was scaled up to be available in all regions in 2012, although up-to-date data on coverage is not available. A 2015 review of the scheme found that pastoralist households purchasing IBLI before the shock recover faster from shock-induced asset losses than comparable non-insured households, with policyholders tending to have larger herds 1–2 years after the shock studied, although with the effect declining thereafter.[79]

Quantifying the Protection Gap

The combined AAL associated with floods and earthquakes is estimated to be under $25 million per annum. Indirect losses might increase this by a further $6 million, but these numbers are excluded from the base case assessment. Precise data on the extent to which insurance might cover these losses is difficult to ascertain. Property insurance premiums, as a percentage of the AALs associated with these two perils, are among the highest of any country in the CAREC region, and property insurance by default covers both earthquake and flood risk. However, the relatively large premium payment of the losses associated with these perils may partly reflect the disproportionate importance of other perils in Mongolia. In the base case, it is assumed that 20% of the losses associated in Ulaanbaatar and 3% of the losses experienced elsewhere in the country are insured. This amounts to insurance covering just under 5% of the total losses caused by these risks.

---

[77]   A *dzud* is a multifaceted disaster event characterized by a summer drought, in which insufficient fodder is available for stockpiling, followed by heavy winter snow and abnormally low temperatures.

[78]   Data taken from Swiss Re Sigma, https://www.swissre.com/institute/research/sigma-research/World-insurance-series.html. Insurance density refers to the premia amount divided by population.

[79]   V. Bertram-Huemmer and K. Kraehnert. 2015. Does index insurance help households recover from disaster? Evidence from IBLI Mongolia. *DIW Discussion Papers* No. 1515. Berlin: Deutsches Institut für Wirtschaftsforschung (DIW). https://www.econstor.eu/bitstream/10419/122303/1/840001517.pdf.

Finally, it is assumed that $26 million might be available for the various contingency and reserve funds set up by the government, equal to the amount made available from the Government Reserve Fund for disaster events in 2013 and 2014. These assumptions imply that the funding available is just sufficient to cover the annual losses that might be experienced on average, as shown in Figure 25. Correspondingly, as shown in Table 9, it would only take a 1 in 10-year flood event to cause the risk retention mechanisms less insurance provision to be exhausted if the funds were to cover either both direct and indirect losses or direct losses only. The sharp increase in losses between a 1 in 10-year and 1 in 20-year flood event also means that a 1 in 20-year flood event would be sufficient to exhaust the risk retention mechanisms if their intention was only to cover emergency response costs. The low risks associated with earthquakes in Mongolia mean that only earthquake events more severe than a 1 in 200-year event would cause depletion of the risk retention mechanisms available to the country.

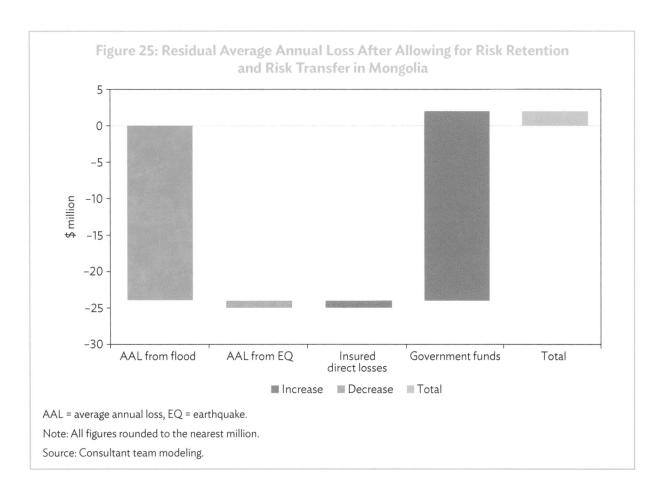

Figure 25: Residual Average Annual Loss After Allowing for Risk Retention and Risk Transfer in Mongolia

AAL = average annual loss, EQ = earthquake.

Note: All figures rounded to the nearest million.

Source: Consultant team modeling.

Table 9: Event Frequency at which Ex Ante Mechanisms Are Exhausted in Mongolia

Event frequency where direct and indirect losses, less (assumed) insured losses, exceed existing ex ante risk retention		Event frequency where direct losses, less (assumed) insured losses, exceed existing ex ante risk retention		Event frequency where estimated emergency response costs exceed current risk retention mechanisms	
Flood	**Earthquake**	**Flood**	**Earthquake**	**Flood**	**Earthquake**
1 in 10	>1 in 200	1 in 10	>1 in 200	1 in 20	>1 in 200

Source: Consultant team modeling.

Ability to Rely on Ex Post Borrowing

The macroeconomic context of the country is weak, implying that reliance on ex post borrowing on the capital markets is unlikely to be feasible. Heavily exposed to commodity price volatility, Mongolia's external debt ratio has risen sixfold over the past decade, with the government debt-to-GDP ratio at 77%,[80] the second highest within the CAREC region, less only than that of Pakistan. It also has one of the lower credit ratings of countries in the CAREC region. Meanwhile, the impact of COVID-19 on Mongolia's finances has been severe. The economy shrunk by 5.3% in 2020, leading to a spike in the government's debt-to-GDP ratio (footnote 79), while government relief efforts—in the form of income support and tax relief—had eroded the fiscal deficit, reversing the trend seen over the past few years of a steadily decreasing debt stock.[81] Figure 26 summarizes.

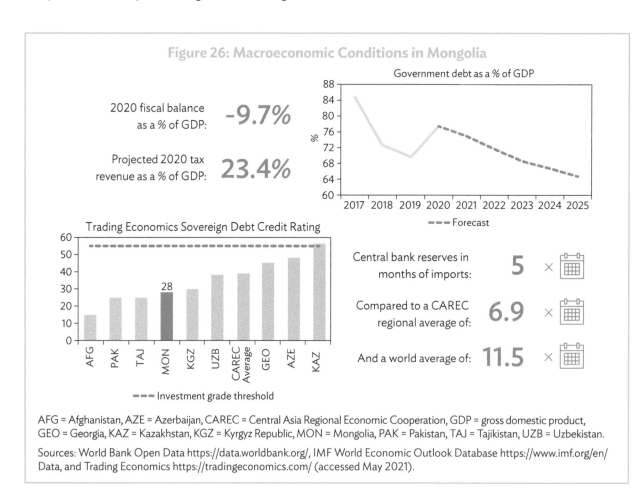

Figure 26: Macroeconomic Conditions in Mongolia

2020 fiscal balance as a % of GDP: **-9.7%**

Projected 2020 tax revenue as a % of GDP: **23.4%**

Government debt as a % of GDP

Trading Economics Sovereign Debt Credit Rating

Central bank reserves in months of imports: **5** ×

Compared to a CAREC regional average of: **6.9** ×

And a world average of: **11.5** ×

AFG = Afghanistan, AZE = Azerbaijan, CAREC = Central Asia Regional Economic Cooperation, GDP = gross domestic product, GEO = Georgia, KAZ = Kazakhstan, KGZ = Kyrgyz Republic, MON = Mongolia, PAK = Pakistan, TAJ = Tajikistan, UZB = Uzbekistan.

Sources: World Bank Open Data https://data.worldbank.org/, IMF World Economic Outlook Database https://www.imf.org/en/Data, and Trading Economics https://tradingeconomics.com/ (accessed May 2021).

The implication of this analysis—that the country is making limited use of insurance mechanisms, only has risk retention mechanisms in place to cover the most frequent events, and has limited access to ex post borrowing options—is corroborated by historic events. Analysis in the country's Disaster Risk Reduction White Paper shows that government expenditures for post-disaster activities have tended to amount to only 4% of the estimated total economic losses over the period 2004–2013. Just under three quarters of these expenditures have been financed from the state reserves identified above, with the remainder coming from budget reallocation. The same report

---

[80]   IMF. *Country Data, Mongolia.* https://www.imf.org/en/Countries/MNG.
[81]   World Bank. 2021. *Mongolia Economy Update.* Washington, DC. February.

notes that the percentage of losses covered increases to 27% when taking into account donations from citizens, international organizations, and NGOs.[82]

Similarly, Mongolia has relied heavily on international assistance to support its COVID-19 response. As with Afghanistan and the Kyrgyz Republic, it is noteworthy that the total international assistance received from countries and international financial institutions, $2.9 billion, is greater than the estimated value of the response measures, $2.2 billion.

Notwithstanding the challenges faced at a sovereign level, the ability of households, including poor households, to bounce back from the impact of moderate disasters is enhanced by high rates of financial inclusion. Of the population, 93% has a bank account, rising to 95% among women. Moreover, there is no notable discrepancy across income groups or between urban and rural populations (footnote 24). These high rates of financial inclusion are helped by the nationally owned XacBank which has 50% of its client base in rural locations.[83]

Social protection measures are also likely to support resilience to disaster events, although they may imply a greater proportion of the losses associated with disaster events end up being absorbed by the state. Ninety-four percent of the population are covered by one or more social insurance, social safety net, unemployment benefit or active labor market programs, rising to 98.7% among the bottom income quintile. This is the highest rate of any of the countries in the CAREC region.[84] The Government of Mongolia has also demonstrated interest in reinforcing existing social protection programs with considerations of shock responsiveness. Since 2019, UNICEF and the government have been implementing a shock responsive social protection (SRSP) pilot in Mongolia. The pilot uses funds from Mongolia's Child Money Programme in the form of emergency cash transfers for livelihoods affected by the annual *dzud*. Consisting of two phases, the pilot targets over 9,500 children in Zavkhan province—which has the heaviest snowfall in the country—by giving households cash assistance to prepare for winter.[85] Two further SRSP projects, supported by ADB, were approved in 2020 and 2021, with financial commitments of $26.4 million and $73.2 million respectively (the former also having a further $5 million loan from the World Bank).[86]

Summary

Mongolia's contingent liabilities from disaster events, especially those associated with floods, are inadequately addressed by its current disaster risk financing strategy. The risk retention mechanisms are only sufficient to cover the emergency response costs associated with frequent events and are likely to be exhausted by a 1 in 10-year flood. Private insurance markets are likely to pick up a very small proportion of the associated losses, and virtually none of the losses outside the capital city. Moreover, the strained fiscal position of the government means that it is unlikely to be able to quickly and easily rely on ex post borrowing to meet the funding needs associated with these disaster events. These challenges are exemplified in the financial challenges that the government has had in responding to historic disasters. At the same time, the country's existing policy framework toward financial inclusion and social protection, some of which are being supported by ADB, may give greater confidence that sovereign-level support will filter down toward those households that are particularly vulnerable.

---

[82]   National Emergency Management Agency. 2017. *2017 White Paper on Disaster Risk Reduction in Mongolia: Summary.* https://www.jica.go.jp/project/mongolia/016/materials/ku57pq0000316w3f-att/2017WhitePaper_Summary_Eng.pdf.

[83]   ADB. 2017. *Supporting Micro, Small, and Medium-Sized Enterprises in Mongolia.* https://www.adb.org/sites/default/files/project-documents/47930/47930-001-xarr-en.pdf.

[84]   World Bank ASPIRE Database. https://www.worldbank.org/en/data/datatopics/aspire/country/mongolia (accessed May 2021).

[85]   UNICEF. *Summary of Shock-Responsive Social Protection Programme Pilot for Rural Children.* https://www.jointsdgfund.org/article/summary-shock-responsive-social-protection-programme-pilot-rural-children.

[86]   ADB. Mongolia: Shock-Responsive Social Protection Project. https://www.adb.org/projects/54214-001/main#project-pds; and ADB. Mongolia: Second Shock-Responsive Social Protection Project. https://www.adb.org/projects/54214-002/main#project-overview.

Pakistan

Flood and Earthquake Risk

Both flood and earthquake risk are significant in Pakistan, shown in Figure 27. Floods are associated with an AAL of around $1.5 billion dollars and earthquakes with an AAL of around $614 million. This rises to $1.6 billion and $644 million with the inclusion of indirect losses. This is the highest absolute amount of loss of any country in the CAREC region and across the two perils direct losses amount to 0.20% of GNI, the fourth-highest losses as a percentage of national income of any country in the region. As Figure 27 shows, floods are expected to cause greater losses than earthquakes for events of the same return for return periods of up to (at least) 1 in 200 years.[87]

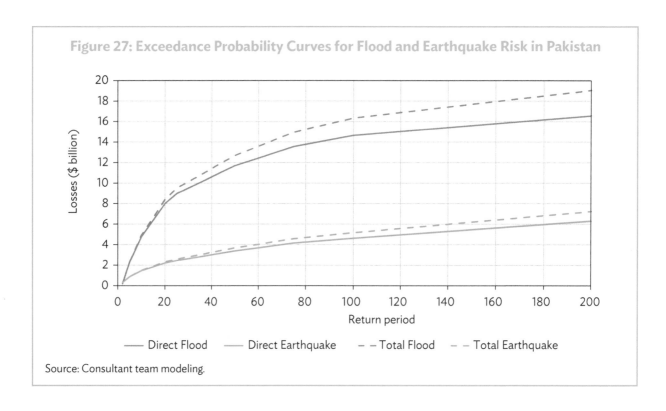

Figure 27: Exceedance Probability Curves for Flood and Earthquake Risk in Pakistan

Source: Consultant team modeling.

Reflecting the large absolute population of the country, the loss of life associated with these risks is also substantial. Earthquakes are expected to be associated with an average annual loss of life of 863 deaths, around seven times higher than the country with the next highest expected loss of life from this peril. The number of people expected to be severely affected by earthquakes is just under 165,000, also the highest figure in the region. Floods are expected to cause a further 234 deaths each year with more than 678,000 people expected to be severely affected by flooding. Respectively, these are the second highest and highest numbers for this peril in the CAREC region.

It is striking that the proportion of the population living in multidimensional poverty is much higher in Pakistan than in many other countries in the CAREC region, with more than 50% of the population in Balochistan, Khyber Pakhtunkhwa and Sindh meeting this classification. While there is a general negative correlation between the direct losses caused by floods and earthquakes and the proportion of people living in multidimensional poverty,

---

[87]   It is only for events of a return period of 1 in 800 years that earthquakes cause greater loss than floods (not shown in Figure 27).

Sindh is noteworthy for ranking relatively highly on both metrics (Figure 28). The same broad pattern emerges from considering the relationship between multidimensional poverty and expected loss of life, although when considering this correlation, Khyber Pakhtunkhwa stands out more as a "hot spot."

There is a strong agricultural focus to economic activity in Khyber Pakhtunkhwa, accounting for around 40% of the province's labor force, with key crops including wheat, maize, and sugar beet. Industrial activity is dominated by SMEs and focuses heavily on textiles and apparel as well as food, beverages, and tobacco flour mills; though leather, gems, and marble mining can be found in specific parts of the province.[88] In Sindh, most of the poverty is found in rural and semi-urban areas (i.e., outside of Karachi) with farming and agribusinesses as particularly important sectors for SMEs.[89]

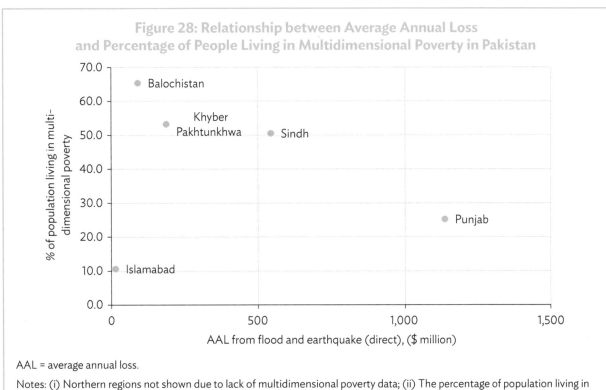

Figure 28: Relationship between Average Annual Loss
and Percentage of People Living in Multidimensional Poverty in Pakistan

AAL = average annual loss.

Notes: (i) Northern regions not shown due to lack of multidimensional poverty data; (ii) The percentage of population living in multidimensional poverty in Khyber Pakhtunkhwa is calculated as a population weighted average for this indicator value for the Federally Administered Tribal Area and Khyber Pakhtunkhwa.

Sources: Consultant team modeling and Oxford Poverty and Human Development Initiative.

Risk Retention and Insurance Penetration

The National Disaster Management Act of 2010 established a National Disaster Management Fund and separate disaster management funds to be administered by each provincial government. These are intended to cover spending on items such as shelter, food, drinking water, medical cover, etc. However, ADB reports that "significant work remains to be accomplished in operationalization of the funds, adequate provision of financing mechanisms,

88   https://smeda.org/index.php?option=com_phocadownload&view=category&id=1:khyber-pakhtunkhwa-district-economic-profiles&Itemid=1024.
89   International Trade Centre. 2020. *Competitiveness of Rural MSMEs and their Resilience to COVID-19 Crisis: Evidence from Sindh, Pakistan.*
       https://intracen.org/media/file/9608.

and standardization of procedures across provinces."[90] It reports that the federal government typically only has limited contingency funding of around $15 million–$20 million to respond to national emergencies while a 2019 World Bank paper reports that the federal fund has $10.6 million.[91] It is not clear how much more might be available to provincial governments.

With support from ADB,[92] a disaster risk financing unit has been established under the National Disaster Risk Management Fund (note it is different from the National Disaster Management Fund discussed above). This unit is responsible for the improved management of natural hazard risks and has set itself three targets:[93]

(i)   **To analyze disaster risks based on identification of hazards and risks.** This includes the quantification of expected disaster costs and the preparation of disaster risk management strategies based on the analysis. To support this, a NatCat model is being developed to cover earthquake, fluvial floods, droughts, and tropical cyclones. This is being developed by the Pakistan Space and Upper Atmosphere Research Commission (SUPARCO).

(ii)   **To develop a strategy for disaster risk financing and the transfer of risk.** It is expected that the strategy will "identify appropriate tools for each layer of risk, based on multi-hazard loss curves and taking into account the scale of funding required for each layer of risk, the speed with which disbursement of funding is required, and the relative cost-effectiveness of alternative instruments for specific layers of loss."

(iii) **To develop and pilot disaster risk finance instruments.** The website identifies that two disaster risk finance solutions (instruments) will be developed, and one will be piloted. The status of the work of this unit, or the instruments that will be developed or piloted, is not clear. The last reported activity related to disaster risk finance is that a national consultative workshop was held in July 2019 in Dubai.

Penetration of retail insurance is low, both by comparison to other CAREC countries and more generally. In 2015, reports suggest only 1.9% of the population held any form of insurance policy.[94] The nonlife insurance penetration rate is estimated to be 0.3% as of 2019, and insurance density estimated at $4/person (footnote 30). These low rates reflect security challenges, widespread poverty, and constrained access to capital for lower income households.

Forty-four percent of the nonlife market is composed of property insurance premiums. Of these policies, it is estimated that around 70% of property policies include cover for earthquakes and other atmospheric disturbances, such as cyclones (footnote 47). There is little information available on the extent to which property insurances policies include cover for floods, but ADB reports that insured losses from the 2010 floods amounted to just 1% of total losses from this event (footnote 89). World Bank reports suggest that only around 1%–2% of residential properties in the country are insured against disasters (footnote 90). Further, despite insurance of public assets being mandatory, ADB reports that only 30% of public assets are insured according to the State Life Insurance Corporation, and that these are only insured during the construction phase (footnote 89).

[90]   ADB. 2019. *The Enabling Environment for Disaster Risk Financing in Pakistan: Country Diagnostic Assessment.* https://www.adb.org/publications/pakistan-environment-disaster-risk-financing.

[91]   World Bank. 2019. *Options to Strengthen Disaster Risk Financing in Pakistan.* https://documents1.worldbank.org/curated/en/858541586180590633/pdf/Options-to-Strengthen-Disaster-Risk-Financing-in-Pakistan.pdf.

[92]   ADB. Pakistan: National Disaster Risk Management Fund. https://www.adb.org/projects/50316-001/main.

[93]   NDRMF. *DRF Introduction.* https://www.ndrmf.pk/drf-introduction/.

[94]   J. Miow. 2015. *Pakistan – Growth Potential of a Nascent Insurance Market.* https://www.peak-re.com/insights/pakistan-growth-potential-of-a-nascent-insurance-market/.

However, recent government-supported housing schemes are encouraging the take up of property insurance. The Naya Pakistan Housing Programme aims to construct 5 million affordable housing units for Pakistanis, with eligible citizens benefiting from subsidies to ensure affordability. Reports suggest that 135,000 units are being developed in the first part of the scheme.[95] Under the scheme, developers are required to take out insurance up to the full value of the property in the case of apartments and up to the construction cost value in the case of houses.[96] However, it is unclear whether this is just required for the period of construction or also while the house is occupied.

There have also been some attempts to support agricultural insurance.[97] Under the national Crop Loan Insurance Scheme those who use agricultural production loans from banks or microfinance institutions are required to purchase the insurance. The policy insures against disasters but only pays out if crop losses are greater than 50% of total yield. The Pakistani government provides a 100% subsidy for small farmers and 50% of premiums for farmers with landholdings 5 to 25 acres. In 2018, a pilot project in Punjab region introduced an index-based subsidized agricultural insurance product which has rapidly spread in popularity, issuing 227,000 insurance contracts in 2019. By 2023, it is expected that 3.5 million farmers could be covered under the scheme (footnote 96).

Quantifying the Protection Gap

The analysis uses the results from the modeling undertaken as part of this project as presented in Figure 27. The AAL (direct losses only) from flood events is estimated at $1.5 billion and from earthquakes at $614 million. In terms of the extent to which insurance might cover these losses, the analysis assumes that 1% of the losses from flood events may be covered by insurance, in line with the ADB analysis. It is assumed that a higher proportion of the losses from earthquakes might be covered by insurance based on market reports that 70% of property insurance policies cover earthquakes. The base-case analysis assumes that 4% o losses from earthquakes might be covered. Given the relative losses associated with flood and earthquakes, these assumptions imply that around 2% of the total losses from the two perils are covered by insurance.

The analysis also takes account of the funding available in the risk retention mechanisms. It is assumed that $20 million might be available toward the top end of the reported funding to allow for an unknown amount of resources that may be available in provincial disaster risk funds. Nonetheless, the analysis shows that current disaster risk finance resources are woefully inadequate to meet the costs and losses that are expected to be caused by disaster events each year (Figure 29). Indeed, the assumptions regarding risk retention and risk transfer imply sufficient funding to only cover 3% of the AAL, leaving a residual "unfunded" AAL of around $2.1 billion (97%). Consistent with this, current disaster risk finance resources are insufficient to cover the total losses, the direct losses or even the emergency response costs associated with events of all frequencies (Table 10).

95   Zameen Blog. https://www.zameen.com/blog/naya-pakistan-housing-program-latest-updates.html.
96   Naya Pakistan Housing Program. *SBP Prudential Regulations.* https://www.sbp.org.pk/publications/prudential/FAQs-PrudentialRegulationsHousin gFinance.pdf.
97   World Bank. 2018. *Assessing the Potential for Large Scale Agricultural Crop and Livestock Insurance.* June. https://documents1.worldbank.org/ curated/en/906921547616572396/pdf/133553-WP-P162446-PUBLIC-Punjab-Crop-Insurance-Web.pdf.

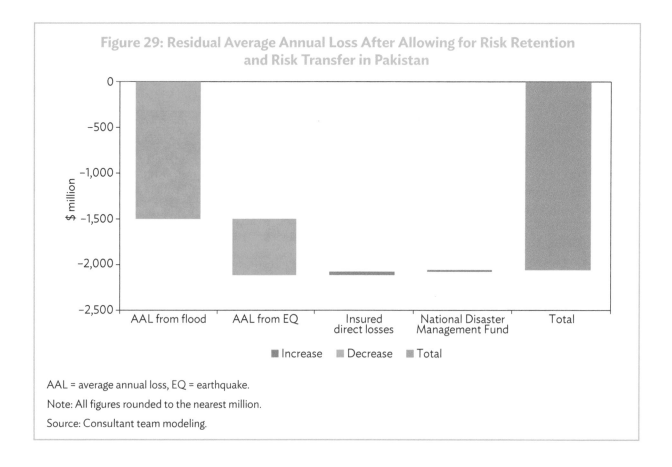

Figure 29: Residual Average Annual Loss After Allowing for Risk Retention and Risk Transfer in Pakistan

AAL = average annual loss, EQ = earthquake.

Note: All figures rounded to the nearest million.

Source: Consultant team modeling.

Table 10: Event Frequency at which Ex Ante Mechanisms Are Exhausted in Pakistan

Event frequency where direct and indirect losses, less (assumed) insured losses, exceed existing ex ante risk retention		Event frequency where direct losses, less (assumed) insured losses, exceed existing ex ante risk retention		Event frequency where estimated emergency response costs exceed current risk retention mechanisms	
Flood	Earthquake	Flood	Earthquake	Flood	Earthquake
All	All	All	All	All	All

Source: Consultant team modeling.

Ability to Rely on Ex Post Borrowing

Even before the impact of the COVID-19 crisis, Pakistan was in a challenging fiscal position with limited fiscal space. It suffers from both high levels of public debt and a large fiscal deficit with the government already borrowing heavily to finance day to day expenditure. Its credit rating is among the lowest of any country in the CAREC region. As well as the expected impact of COVID-19 on the size of the economy—estimated to have contracted by 1.5% in the 2020 financial year[98]—the pandemic has interrupted the government's fiscal consolidation efforts as part of the IMF-Extended Fund Facility. This interruption has exacerbated fiscal imbalances and further damages the government's finances. On recent occasions, Pakistan has had to reach bilateral arrangements with creditors to

---

[98]   World Bank. 2021. *The World Bank in Pakistan.* https://www.worldbank.org/en/country/pakistan/overview.

extend repayment of maturing debt. The IMF has assessed the overall risk of debt distress in the country as high and its debt carrying capacity as weak.[99] Figure 30 summarizes.

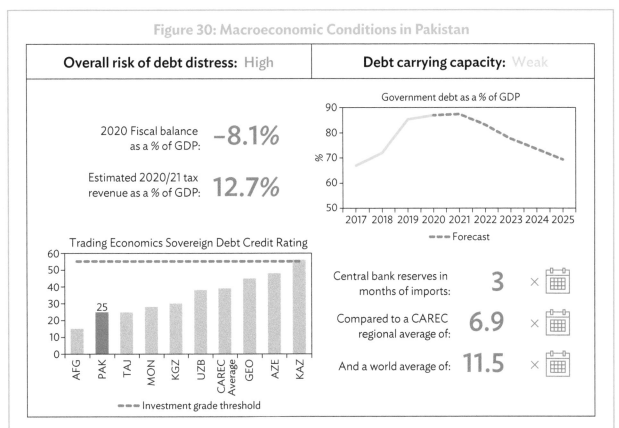

Figure 30: Macroeconomic Conditions in Pakistan

AFG = Afghanistan, AZE = Azerbaijan, CAREC = Central Asia Regional Economic Cooperation, GDP = gross domestic product, GEO = Georgia, KAZ = Kazakhstan, KGZ = Kyrgyz Republic, MON = Mongolia, PAK = Pakistan, TAJ = Tajikistan, UZB = Uzbekistan.

Sources: World Bank Open Data https://data.worldbank.org/, IMF World Economic Outlook Database https://www.imf.org/en/Data, and Trading Economics https://tradingeconomics.com/ (accessed May 2021).

Financing challenges are also strongly evident for individuals and households, with Pakistan suffering from some of the lowest rates of financial inclusion in the world. Less than a quarter of the population has a bank account, and only 7% of the female population do so, implying some of the greatest gender inequality in the region (footnote 24). There have been, however, a number of recent efforts to improve financial inclusion with, for example, the creation of the Pakistan Microfinance Investment Company in 2018 and the Digitization of its Benazir Income Support Programme (BISP) in 2010, which helped as many as 6 million women move to a digital savings platform.[100] Meanwhile, the Aga Khan Foundation has previously led a series of initiatives in the north of the country, providing female-targeted literacy and community training, along with "Women Only" markets and organizations.[101]

Neither are social protection programs likely to be particularly effective in protecting the most vulnerable populations following a disaster. According to the latest data, only 26% of the bottom income quintile are covered by social protection or labor programs (footnote 64). Pakistan's main system of support is an unconditional cash transfer for 5 million

99   IMF. 2019. *Pakistan. Request for an Arrangement under the Extended Fund Facility – Debt Sustainability Analysis.* Washington, DC.
100   S. Nishtar. 2020. *COVID-19 and the Pursuit of Financial Inclusion in Pakistan.* https://www.weforum.org/agenda/2020/06/covid-19-pursuit-financial-inclusion-pakistan/.
101   AKRSP. *Social Pillar.* http://akrsp.org.pk/index.php/programmes/social-pillar/.

people through the BISP, which is primarily focused on the poor, rural, female population. Recent research has revealed challenges with the scheme resulting from disruptions in payment frequency and insufficient funding.[102] In recent years, the government has introduced the Ehsaas Strategy, an initiative that combines BISP cash transfers with skills training, financial inclusion, and other measures to address poverty, while the Kamyab Jawan program also provides support for young entrepreneurs. Conditional cash transfers to encourage school-age children to return to school were rolled out on a national level in late 2020.[103] The effectiveness of these additional initiatives is not yet clear.

However, there are innovative approaches to make social protection measures more shock-responsive, which may enhance households' financial resilience. The current extent of shock-responsiveness in social protection varies by province, with Punjab and Khyber Pakhtunkhwa leading the way through policies that acknowledge the relationship between social protection and covariate disaster management. The provincial government of Punjab has introduced a cash-based flood response program, while in Khyber Pakhtunkhwa, the provincial government provides cash transfers to internally displaced people to mitigate the impact of displacement under conflict. The ongoing process of adopting a national social protection policy framework—which intends to streamline different initiatives—is expected to facilitate more shock-responsive social protection programming, with the BISP having been identified by some stakeholders for offering potential for comprehensive SRSP operationalization in Pakistan.[104] Ehsaas Tahafuz, which forms part of the Ehsaas Strategy, is Pakistan's first "shock-oriented" initiative that assist the vulnerable population in covering "catastrophic" health expenditures.[105]

Summary

There is an urgent need to enhance the current disaster risk finance approach in Pakistan. Risk retention mechanisms are insufficient to cover the losses associated with even the most frequent of flood and earthquake events, while private insurance solutions for these risks have achieved only minimal market penetration. These challenges are compounded by a challenging external financing context at the sovereign level, making it difficult to access debt quickly and cheaply after a disaster, and low levels of financial inclusion that exacerbate the vulnerability to disaster events of many in Pakistan. Previous disaster events illustrate the challenges that Pakistan faces: for example, floods in 2010 and 2015 caused an estimated PRs32.6 billion ($326 million) losses to farmers in Punjab. To support the affected farmers, the Government of Pakistan provided PRs6.7 billion ($67 million)—amounting to only 18.5% of the required amount.[106]

There would appear to be a need to increase the coverage and depth of the existing risk retention instruments for high frequency events, through enhanced functioning of the national and provincial disaster management funds. This could be complemented with the use of risk transfer instruments that might support either the emergency response cost and/or the support the reconstruction of assets damaged or destroyed by lower frequency, higher intensity events. These actions are consistent with the identified workplan of the Disaster Risk Financing Unit of the National Disaster Risk Management Fund.

[102] Pakistan Institute of Development Economics (PIDE). 2020. *Unconditional Cash Transfer and Poverty Alleviation in Pakistan*. https://www.pide.org.pk/pdf/Policy-Viewpoint-18.pdf.
[103] Government of Pakistan, Poverty Alleviation and Social Safety Division. 2020. Dr. Sania addresses a news conference to unveil details about nationwide rollout of massively reformed Waseela-e-Taleem, under the Ehsaas umbrella. *News Release*. 12 November. https://www.pass.gov.pk/NewsDetailWerFf65%5ES23d$gHbd80ca13-940e-4ef6-bd3a-f2987dee80850ecFf65%5ES23d$Pd.
[104] C. Watson et al. 2017. *Shock-responsive social protection systems research. Case study: Pakistan*. https://assets.publishing.service.gov.uk/media/59e0d4f7ed915d6aadcdaf04/OPM-Case-Study-2017-SRSP-Pakistan.pdf.
[105] S. Shaheen. 2021. Ehsaas Tahafuz Project Management Unit launched. *Business Recorder*. 22 January. https://www.brecorder.com/news/40054582/ehsaas-tahafuz-project-management-unit-launched.
[106] World Bank. 2019. *Options to Strengthen Disaster Risk Financing in Pakistan*. https://documents1.worldbank.org/curated/en/858541586180590633/pdf/Options-to-Strengthen-Disaster-Risk-Financing-in-Pakistan.pdf.

People's Republic of China: Inner Mongolia Autonomous Region and Xinjiang Uygur Autonomous Region

Flood and Earthquake Risk

Both flood and earthquake risk are significant in Inner Mongolia Autonomous Region (IMAR) and Xinjiang Uygur Autonomous Region (XUAR). In IMAR, direct AAL from the two perils in combination are equivalent to around $369 million, or 0.09% of GDP. Including indirect losses, this rises to around $402 million (0.10% of GDP).[107] In XUAR, both absolute and proportionate losses are somewhat greater: $390 million and 0.12% of GDP excluding indirect losses, and $442 million and 0.14% including indirect losses. In IMAR, flood events with a return period more frequent than ~1 in 50 years cause greater losses than earthquake events with the same return period. In XUAR, earthquakes cause more losses than floods at all return periods. Figure 31 and Figure 32 provide more details.

In line with the higher direct and indirect losses suffered in XUAR compared to IMAR, it also suffers a greater average annual loss of life: 89 lives as opposed to 48 lives. The higher mortality seen in XUAR is driven by earthquakes, which account for 84 of the 89 average lives lost. On average, across the two provinces, just under 12,500 people are expected to be severely affected by earthquakes each year while just over 93,000 will be severely affected by flooding in an average year, around two thirds of whom live in IMAR.

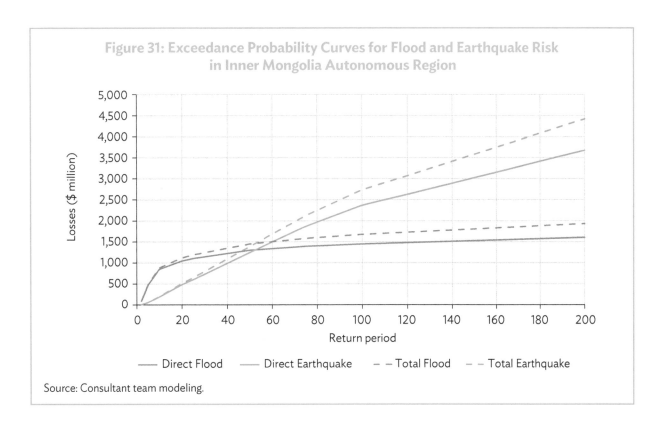

Figure 31: Exceedance Probability Curves for Flood and Earthquake Risk in Inner Mongolia Autonomous Region

Source: Consultant team modeling.

---

[107]   In contrast to other jurisdictions, losses are expressed relative to GDP in the region in 2019 international dollars, as GNI data at the provincial level in the PRC is not available.

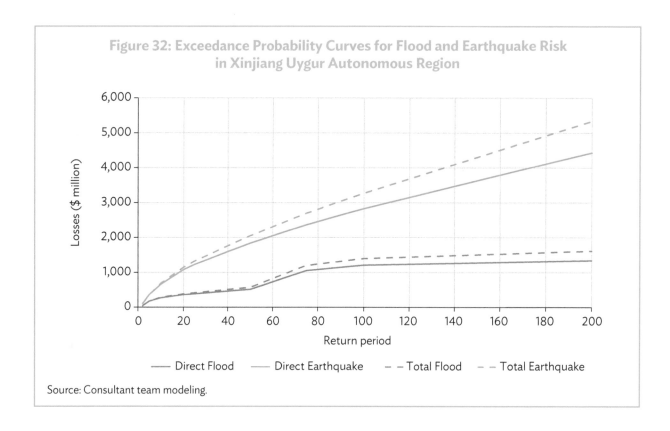

Figure 32: Exceedance Probability Curves for Flood and Earthquake Risk
in Xinjiang Uygur Autonomous Region

Source: Consultant team modeling.

Risk Retention and Insurance Penetration

Disaster risk financing responsibilities in the PRC are shared between national and provincial government. The national government is responsible for Level I (extraordinarily severe disaster events); responsibility for Level II (major disaster events) and Level III (larger disaster events) are shared between local and national governments; while Level IV (ordinary disaster events) are met by local governments. There are four main categories of disaster relief funds that are available to meet the costs of disaster events:[108]

(i)   reserve budgets for defined stipulated emergency and disaster functions;

(ii) under the 1994 Budget Law, all levels of governments are expected to save 1%–3% of their annual expenditures for unexpected events, including disaster events. However, it has not been possible to identify the amount of funds in IMAR and XUAR associated with this provision. Moreover, each province relies heavily on central transfer payments for its budgetary needs;

(iii) the Fiscal Budget Stabilization Fund which had a balance of CNY527 billion (~$80 billion) at the end of 2019; and

(iv) special purpose funds such as the Central Disaster Relief Fund, which had around CNY12 billion in 2020 ($1.85 billion), and the Central Agricultural Production Disaster Prevention and Relief Fund, which has around CNY6 billion to CNY8 billion annually ($0.9 billion–$1.2 billion).

To help improve its ability to cover the losses associated with disaster events, the state-owned reinsurer China Re issued its first catastrophe bond in 2015. This is understood to provide cover for around $50 million of earthquake risk, with an indemnity trigger.[109]

---

108   ADB. (undated). *From Pandemic to Greater Resilience: Managing Disaster Risks.* Manila.
109   Artemis. 2015. *Panda Re Ltd. 2015-1, the first cat bond covering Chinese perils.* https://www.artemis.bm/news/panda-re-ltd-2015-1-the-first-cat-bond-covering-chinese-perils/.

Insurance penetration in both IMAR and XUAR is high, although this is driven largely by agricultural insurance. In IMAR, nonlife insurance penetration is 1.24% and insurance density is $126; the equivalent figures in XUAR are 1.66% and $128. These high rates are driven by what is intended to be compulsory crop insurance through the China Agricultural Policy Insurance Program. In 2012, 95% of farms in IMAR were insured through this program, while livestock insurance is also intended to be compulsory.[110] The penetration of agricultural insurance in these two provinces matches national experience where agricultural insurance has grown rapidly, supported by premium subsidies. The PRC is the second-largest agriculture insurance market in the world, with premiums reaching almost $11 billion in 2019, with the market growing sixfold since 2010.[111]

By contrast, buildings insurance for flood and earthquake risk is less extensive, although specific data for IMAR and XUAR is difficult to ascertain:

(i)   Earthquake cover is an optional extension for property insurance, with cover typically limited to 70%–80% of the sum insured, depending on contract type. While there is no data available for IMAR specifically, market data collected by Willis Towers Watson suggests that in the 2008 Eastern Sichuan earthquake, insured losses were only 0.2% of total economic losses. Similarly, a report by Swiss Re on the impact that earthquakes may have on the credit risks faced by banks states: "With no known insurance solutions for default risk in operation, the absolute losses for the modeled credit assets are assumed to represent the protection gap."[112]

(ii)   Market reports suggest that flood insurance for properties in rural areas in the PRC is almost zero. However, agriculture insurance means that some of the losses associated with floods in rural areas are covered. Across different (urban and rural) locations in the PRC, insured losses as a percentage of total losses from recent flood events have ranged from around 2% to 5.2%.[113]

In 2015, the government established the Urban and Rural Residential Earthquake Catastrophe Insurance Pool to encourage uptake of homeowner earthquake insurance, including in XUAR. As of 2018, the pool encompassed 45 insurers (footnote 111). XUAR is considered a medium risk territory and it is expected the pool will have a significant presence there.[114] However, it has not been possible to ascertain the impact that this pool has had on insurance penetration. By contrast, IMAR is considered a low-risk territory (footnote 113) and it is not expected that the pool will have a significant presence.

Quantifying the Protection Gap

A quantification of the protection gap in IMAR and XUAR is difficult due to the absence of two pieces of data. First, it has not been possible to source information on the amount of resources saved by the XUAR and IMAR provincial governments for disaster protection. Second, the protection gap would depend on the extent to which the national funds (such as the Central Disaster Relief Fund and Fiscal Budget Stabilization Fund) might be able to meet the contingent liabilities associated with all the PRC provinces—as this would determine whether the "fair share" of these national funds would be sufficient to meet the losses that might be experienced in these two provinces. A wide assessment of flood and earthquake risk in the PRC is beyond the scope of this work.

---

[110]   Y. Zhao, Z. Chai, M. Delgado, and P. Preckel. 2016. An empirical analysis of the effect of crop insurance on farmers' income: Results from Inner Mongolia in China. *China Agricultural Economic Review* 8(2): pp. 299–313.

[111]   AIR Worldwide. 2020. *Agriculture Risk in China.* https://www.air-worldwide.com/blog/posts/2020/11/agricultural-risk-in-china/.

[112]   Swiss Re Institute. 2018. *The earthquake protection gap facing China's commercial banks: on shaky grounds.* https://www.swissre.com/dam/jcr:aa973480-490e-4f23-938b-bc11ba95b0d7/EQ_protection_gap_china.pdf.

[113]   July 2016 Yangtze River flood - 2.0%, July 2012 Beijing flood - 2.3%, 2007 Huahie and Yangtze Rivers flood - 5.2%. Source: Willis Towers Watson market reports.

[114]   Ye Wei, Qi Wang, Chunliang Xiu, Nan Wang. 2015. Featured graphic. An Earthquake risk map of China, *Environment and Planning.* https://journals.sagepub.com/doi/pdf/10.1068/a140641g.

Ability to Rely on Ex Post Borrowing

Both IMAR and XUAR rely heavily on transfers from the central government. In 2019, IMAR's general budgetary revenue, composed of tax and nontax revenues, was equal to only 40% of total budgetary expenditure.[115] In XUAR, in 2019, the equivalent figure was 30%. The remaining shortfall was met by transfers from central government and the issuance of debt, although the precise balance is unclear.[116]

The debt position of both provinces is likely to be concerning, although specific details are unclear. According to the PRC's National Bureau of Statistics, IMAR held total debts equal to 9.7% of its 2019 gross regional product while in XUAR total debt was equal to around 19.2% (footnote 115).

However, at the national level the PRC's strong economic growth, high domestic savings rate and investment grade credit rating supports XUAR's and IMAR's credit profile. Historical experience suggests that this is likely to be the main way in which the contingent liabilities associated with severe events would be met in either province. For example, a wide analysis in the PRC found that the explicit ex ante financing measures have only covered 2%–7% of the estimated direct economic losses from disaster events over the period 1998–2017. Using the earthquake in Wenchuan as a specific example, the analysis shows that the pre-defined budgetary measures (in other words, the ex ante measures) covered $13.6 billion of the direct economic losses of $120.7 billion, with the remainder of the economic losses met through bank loans, Ministry of Finance support beyond the normal budget, and an unanticipated contribution from 19 provincial governments to provide 1% of their fiscal expenditures for contribution to Wenchuan for 3 years (footnote 107).

For households, comparable statistics to those used for sovereign countries elsewhere in this report are not available for either XUAR or IMAR. However, XUAR and IMAR rank fourth and third lowest respectively in the University of Peking's 2018 financial inclusion index.[117] In XUAR, three quarters of females have used a banking service, falling to 52% in IMAR.[118] It is plausible that this implies a higher level of financial inclusion than in many other jurisdictions within the CAREC region.

Summary

It is difficult to assess the protection gap for XUAR and IMAR that is comparable to that of the sovereign countries elsewhere in the CAREC region. On the one hand, the level of risk, especially in XUAR, is relatively high, property insurance penetration is limited, and the ability of the provincial governments, acting unilaterally, to quickly and easily finance contingent liabilities through new debt issuance may be difficult. On the other hand, both provinces can make use both of the explicit ex ante disaster risk financing measures of the central government, as well as its extensive ability to arrange financing ex post.

It is plausible that the most attractive way to support disaster risk finance in these provinces would be through making improvements in the PRC's overall disaster risk financing arrangements and, in particular, its current large reliance on ex post measures. This might be complemented by facilitating the roll out of flood and earthquake insurance for individual property owners.

---

[115] National Bureau of Statistics. 2020. IMAR. http://data.stats.gov.cn/search.htm?s=内蒙古财政收入.
[116] National Bureau of Statistics. 2020. XUAR. http://data.stats.gov.cn/search.htm?s=新疆财政收入.
[117] Institute of Digital Finance, Peking University. 2019. *The Peking University Digital Financial Inclusion Index of China (2011-2018)*. https://en.idf.pku. edu.cn/docs/20190610145822397835.pdf.
[118] Md. Hasan, L. Yajuan, and A. Mahmud. 2020. *Regional Development of China's Inclusive Finance through Financial Technology*. SAGE Open. January. doi:10.1177/2158244019901252.

Tajikistan

Flood and Earthquake Risk

Tajikistan faces significant flood and earthquake risk. AAL from floods is estimated to be around $61 million while the AAL for earthquakes is over $63 million. These amounts increase to $114 million and $165 million when indirect losses are included. The combined direct AAL is equivalent to around 0.32% of Tajikistan's GNI, rising to 0.73% when including indirect losses. This is the second-highest proportion for any CAREC jurisdiction. As Figure 33 shows, the direct losses caused by 1 in 50-year floods and earthquakes are broadly equivalent. For events with more frequent return periods, floods cause greater losses than earthquakes, for events with less frequent return periods, earthquakes cause greater losses. Indirect losses from events in Tajikistan are expected to be particularly high compared to other countries in the CAREC region. This reflects the high interest rate in the country, suggesting that capital is scarce and hence that the capital that has been invested is particularly productive, implying greater indirect losses when it is destroyed by disasters.

There are also human losses associated with each peril. On average, floods are expected to cause around 45 deaths each year and earthquakes are expected to cause 37 deaths. Each year, on average more than 17,500 people are expected to be severely affected by floods and more than 9,000 are expected to be severely affected by earthquakes.

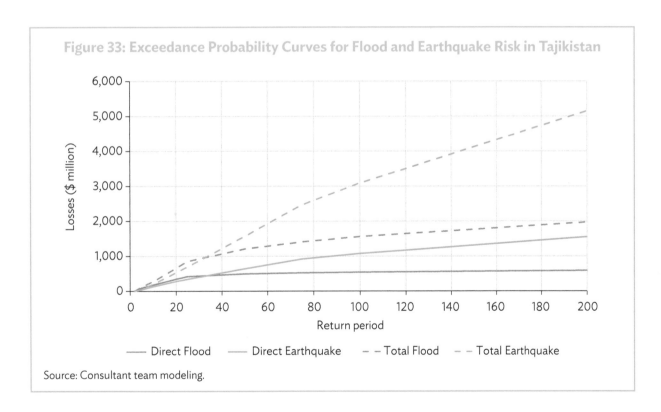

Figure 33: Exceedance Probability Curves for Flood and Earthquake Risk in Tajikistan

Source: Consultant team modeling.

For provinces, there is a clear positive correlation between AALs and average number of lives lost and the proportion of people living in multidimensional poverty. The province of Khatlon is a particular hot spot, with the two perils expected to result in AALs of around $63 million, around 75% of which are from floods, at the same time that more than 10% of the population is living in multidimensional poverty. Forty deaths from earthquakes and floods may be expected each year in this province as well, more than three times higher than in the province with the next greatest number of deaths, Sughd. Figure 34 provides more detail. Economic activity in Khatlon is dominated by primary agriculture and some agribusiness, especially cotton (both raw cotton and cotton fiber) with previous analysis suggesting that Khatlon has a comparative advantage in onions, grapes, and stone fruits, as well as first-level processing potential in fruits and vegetables, skins, wool, and cotton yarn. There is also small amounts of manufacturing of building materials and other light manufacturing.[119]

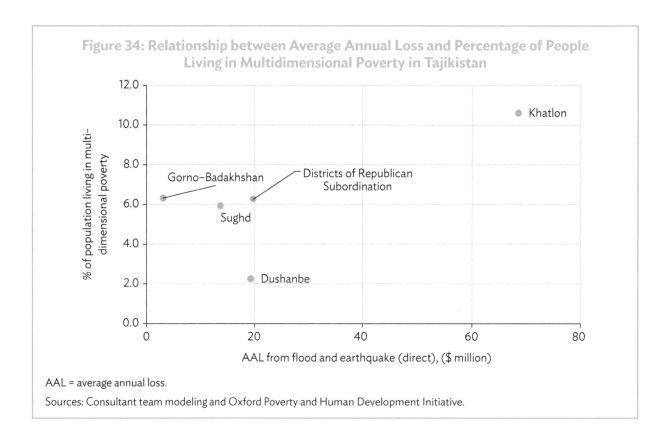

Figure 34: Relationship between Average Annual Loss and Percentage of People Living in Multidimensional Poverty in Tajikistan

AAL = average annual loss.

Sources: Consultant team modeling and Oxford Poverty and Human Development Initiative.

Risk Retention and Insurance Penetration

The response to disasters in Tajikistan is determined by the State Commission of the Government of the Republic of Tajikistan for emergency situations. This body has three responsibilities:[120]

(i)   to prepare proposals for the provision of material and financial support for victims of emergencies;

(ii) to prepare proposals for the allocation of financial, material, and technical resources to address the consequences of emergencies and for implementation of such measures; and

(iii) to prevent and liquidate the consequences of unexpected and urgent emergency situations including the target used of state budget funds.

[119] World Bank. 2013. *Tajikistan: Reinvigorating Growth in the Khatlon Oblast.* https://documents1.worldbank.org/curated/en/677671468339631289/pdf/785250REVISED00atlon0pub08019013web.pdf.

[120] Government Decree Republic of Tajikistan No. 799. 2015. *Regulations on the State Commission of the Government of the Republic of Tajikistan Emergency Management.* http://www.cawater-info.net/bk/dam-safety/files/tj-799-2015.pdf.

There are three main sources of ex ante risk retention instruments that can be used to perform these roles:

(i) **Ex ante budget allocation.** Both the national and local governments include budget line items to provide compensation for people affected by disaster events. In 2009, $0.9 million was allocated in the central budget and $1.6 million allocated in the local budget. In 2010, $1.5 million was allocated in the national budget for this purpose.[121]

(ii) **Local reserve funds.** These are capped at 0.5% of local budgets, but in practice the actual amount within the funds is typically lower. For example, in 2014 the national sum of the amounts planned in the local reserve funds was $3.4 million (and the amount executed was $3.0 million), compared to the maximum possible allocation of $4.5 million. By 2017, the actual amount planned to be held in these reserve funds had fallen to $1.5 million and the amount executed was $1.2 million (footnote 120).

(iii) **Contingent Fund.** The Contingent Fund for the Government of Tajikistan is included in the annual budget with a cap of 0.5% of the total budget revenues. The fund is managed by the Government of Tajikistan, which decides on how to allocate fund resources as a contingency arises. This can include spending on disaster response and rehabilitation but can also include other activities. Between 2008 and 2018, funding had been around $8 million per annum, and was equal to $8.5 million in 2018 (footnote 120).

In total, ex ante sovereign and local government instruments provide for around $11 million–$11.5 million in potential ex ante funding (footnote 57). In addition, there are also small amounts of in-kind support provided in the form of material reserves (e.g., tents, fuel, flour, rice etc.). Beyond these instruments, the government relies on a range of ex post instruments to support disaster finance needs including budget reallocation (except from protected budgets), external borrowing, and donor funding.

The Government of Tajikistan has committed to developing a disaster risk financing strategy. This is being developed by a technical working group led by the Ministry of Finance. The tentative priorities for this strategy are (footnote 120): (i) strengthening disaster risk financing capacity, (ii) establishing a dedicated accruing contingency fund, (iii) improving information on disaster related expenditures, (iv) improving insurance mechanisms, and (v) incentivizing risk reduction.

Tajikistan has one of the smallest insurance markets in the region with an insurance penetration rate of just 0.34% in 2018 (footnote 30). Compulsory property insurance is restricted to perils such as fire and earthquake, with no coverage for floods. Indeed, there is no sophisticated accumulation of flood exposure in Tajikistan, and, aside from some flood modeling undertaken as part of project from the Japan International Cooperation Agency (JICA) to develop a master plan for flood disaster prevention for the Pyanj River,[122] no flood computer models have been developed (footnote 47). Further, while most properties are uninsured against disaster events, the government still often mandates the public insurance company to pay uninsured people affected by a disaster event, effectively converting disaster insurance into a social support mechanism.[123]

Quantifying the Protection Gap

The combined AAL for floods and earthquakes is around $124 million. This rises to $279 million if indirect losses are included but these are excluded from the base-case analysis on the basis that many of these losses will be borne by households and firms rather the government.

---

[121] World Bank. 2019. *Disaster risk finance country note: Tajikistan.* http://documents1.worldbank.org/curated/en/407701574229572325/pdf/Disaster-Risk-Finance-Country-Note-Tajikistan.pdf.

[122] Japan International Cooperation Agency (JICA). 2005. *Scope of Work for the Study of Natural Disaster Prevention in Pyanj River in the Republic of Tajikistan.* https://www.jica.go.jp/english/our_work/social_environmental/archive/pro_asia/pdf/taj02_01.pdf.

[123] World Bank. 2009. *Mitigating the adverse financial effects of natural hazards on the economies of Central Asia.* https://www.unisdr.org/files/11742_MitigatingtheAdverseFinancialEffect.pdf.

In terms of the extent to which insurance might cover these losses, the analysis assumes that there is no insurance cover available for flood risk. For earthquake risk, it is assumed that around 8% of losses might be covered by insurance. This is based on property insurance including earthquake cover being nominally compulsory and observing that property insurance premiums as a percentage of flood and earthquake AAL is 18%, higher than many other countries in the CAREC region. The combined effect of these asumptions is that around 3% of the AAL from flood and earthquakes are assumed to be covered by insurance. The analysis additionally assumes that $12 million of risk retention capacity is available, following the scoping in the preceding section.

The net result is that much of the AAL expected from floods and earthquakes are not financed by any ex ante instruments, with an unfunded residual AAL of $107 million (Figure 35). Correspondingly, even 1 in 5-year flood and earthquake events are expected to exhaust these mechanisms (Table 11). If the mechanisms are expected to cover only emergency response costs, then once again, a 1 in 5-year flood event is expected to exhaust available resources. There is slightly greater protection for the emergency response costs associated with earthquakes but, even for this peril, a 1 in 10-year earthquake event would cause the reserves to be exhausted.

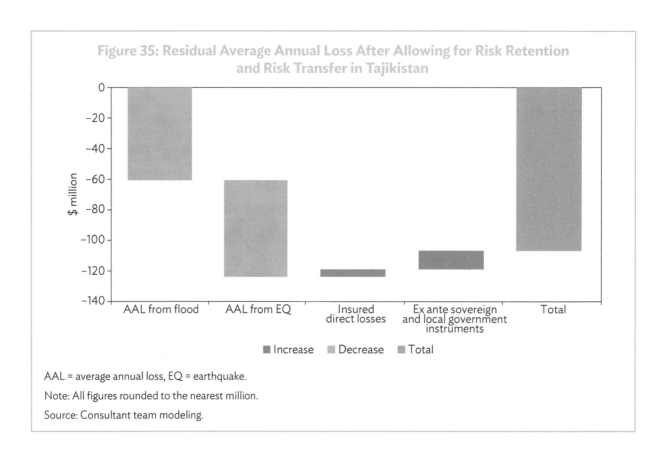

Figure 35: Residual Average Annual Loss After Allowing for Risk Retention and Risk Transfer in Tajikistan

AAL = average annual loss, EQ = earthquake.

Note: All figures rounded to the nearest million.

Source: Consultant team modeling.

Table 11: Event Frequency at which Ex Ante Mechanisms Are Exhausted in Tajikistan

Event frequency where direct and indirect losses, less (assumed) insured losses, exceed existing ex ante risk retention		Event frequency where direct losses, less (assumed) insured losses, exceed existing ex ante risk retention		Event frequency where estimated emergency response costs exceed current risk retention mechanisms	
Flood	**Earthquake**	**Flood**	**Earthquake**	**Flood**	**Earthquake**
1 in 5	1 in 5	1 in 5	1 in 5	1 in 5	1 in 10

Source: Consultant team modeling.

Ability to Rely on Ex Post Borrowing

Exacerbated by the impact of the COVID-19 crisis the Government of Tajikistan is not in a strong position to respond to future disaster events through additional borrowing. The IMF has judged its overall risk of debt distress as high, and it has among the lowest credit ratings of countries in the CAREC region. The COVID-19 crisis has caused remittances to fall and health and social spending to increase. The government ran a fiscal deficit of 4.4% of GDP in 2020, and public sector debt to close to 50% of GDP.[124] In response, the Tajik government has committed to fiscal consolidation over the coming years, but doubts remaining over the viability of its public debt as reflected in its weak credit rating. The economy is especially vulnerable to export shocks and contingent fiscal liabilities, both of which may occur if the country suffers a prolonged COVID-19 impact.

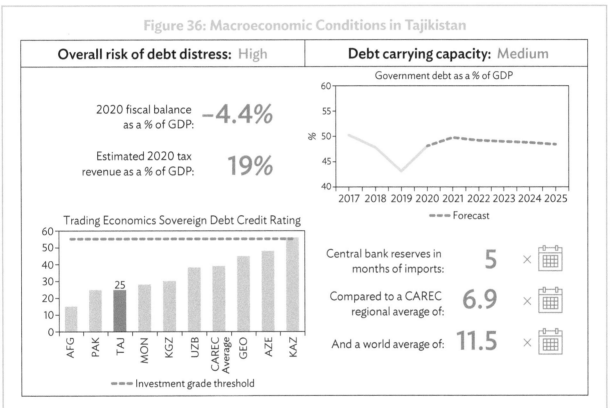

Figure 36: Macroeconomic Conditions in Tajikistan

AFG = Afghanistan, AZE = Azerbaijan, CAREC = Central Asia Regional Economic Cooperation, GDP = gross domestic product, GEO = Georgia, KAZ = Kazakhstan, KGZ = Kyrgyz Republic, MON = Mongolia, PAK = Pakistan, TAJ = Tajikistan, UZB = Uzbekistan.

Sources: World Bank Open Data https://data.worldbank.org/, IMF World Economic Outlook Database https://www.imf.org/en/Data, and Trading Economics https://tradingeconomics.com/ (accessed May 2021).

The reliance on international partners for support in response to disaster events can be seen in the COVID-19 crisis where the country has had to rely heavily on concessional support from international partners totaling $630 million including a $190 million interest-free loan from the IMF; $124 million from the European Union to promote health, education, and social services; and more than $50 million in grants from ADB for health, food security, social protection and micro, small, and medium-sized enterprise support (footnote 71).

[124] IMF and World Bank. 2020. *IMF-World Bank debt sustainability analysis for Tajikistan.* May. https://documents1.worldbank.org/curated/en/209181595281237113/pdf/Tajikistan-Joint-World-Bank-IMF-Debt-Sustainability-Analysis.pdf.

In terms of the financial resilience of households, Tajikistan has made impressive progress in advancing financial inclusion. Whereas in 2011 only 3% of the population had a bank account, this has risen to 47% in 2017. Rates are similar for the rural population as they are for the national average. However, they are lower for women and the poorest two income quintiles (footnote 24). Nonetheless, rates of financial inclusion are lower than those in many other countries in the region. Previous research supported by ADB identifies macroeconomic instability, high poverty rates, and poor access to services as further reasons behind Tajikistan's limited financial inclusion.[125]

Financial resilience to disaster events for individuals and households could also be enhanced by more targeted social protection expenditures. Tajikistan's expenditure on social assistance programs, at 0.8% of GDP in 2018, is the second lowest in the CAREC region, with fewer than 40% of the population receiving any benefit from social and labor market programs.[126] Earlier analysis suggests that only 7% of the poorest quintile households receive energy and cash compensation[127] and only 7.6% of total social assistance expenditure reaches the bottom quintile (footnote 125). There is no evidence that social protection is designed to be shock responsive.

Summary

There are important opportunities to improve arrangements for disaster risk finance in Tajikistan, especially in relation to flood events and more severe earthquakes. Insurance penetration is low and existing risk retention mechanisms are only able to cover either the direct losses or emergency response costs of the most frequent, lowest severity flood events. Flood events that might happen once every 5 years would be sufficient to exhaust current mechanisms which, given Tajikistan's challenging fiscal context, would almost certainly make Tajikistan dependent on support from international development partners. At the level of individuals and households, further improvements in financial inclusion and more targeted (and potentially shock-responsive) social protection could help build financial resilience. This is likely to be particularly valuable in Khatlon, a province which combines high flood and earthquake risk with a relatively large proportion of the population living in multidimensional poverty.

Turkmenistan

Flood and Earthquake Risk

Flood risk is the cause of significantly greater losses than earthquake risks in Turkmenistan. The AAL associated with flood risk is around $140 million (rising to just over $181 million with indirect losses included), whereas that associated with earthquakes is only $11 million (rising to around $20 million with indirect losses included). In combination, the total AAL of around $151 million ($201 million with indirect losses) is equivalent to around 0.18% of GNI, which is the fifth highest across all CAREC countries. As Figure 37 shows, the losses associated with flood risk are greater than the losses associated with earthquake risk at all return periods.

The difference in risks between the two perils is also seen in the average annual loss of life and the average number of people expected to be severely affected. Floods are expected to lead to 173 deaths on average each year (fifth highest among CAREC countries), and severely affect almost 35,000 people, whereas earthquakes are expected to be associated with just 7 deaths (only Mongolia has a lower average loss of life from earthquakes) and severely affect 9,315 people.

125 R. Mogilevskii and S. Asadov. 2018. Financial inclusion, regulation, financial literacy and financial inclusion in Tajikistan. *ADBI Working Paper Series* No 847. https://www.adb.org/sites/default/files/publication/425991/adbi-wp847.pdf.
126 World Bank ASPIRE database. https://www.worldbank.org/en/data/datatopics/aspire/country/tajikistan (accessed May 2021).
127 H. Son. 2014. *Target social protection in Tajikistan where it is needed.* https://blogs.adb.org/blog/target-social-protection-tajikistan-where-it-needed.

Although the proportion of people living in multidimensional poverty is low compared to many other countries in the CAREC region, it is striking that there is a clear positive correlation between the combined AALs from the two perils and the proportion of people living in poverty (Figure 38). A similar relationship exists for the annual average loss of life and poverty incidence. The specific provinces where earthquake and flood risks are high, and poverty is more prevalent are Lebap and Dashoguz.

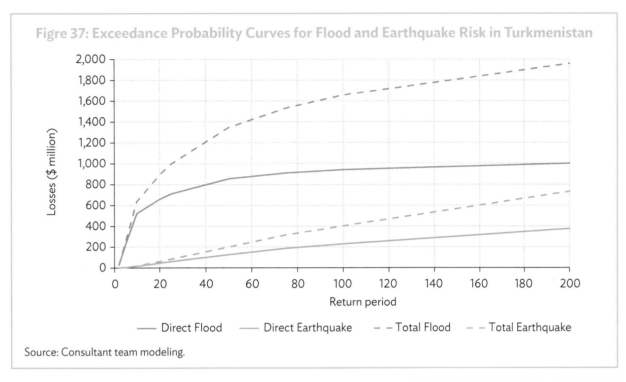

Figre 37: Exceedance Probability Curves for Flood and Earthquake Risk in Turkmenistan

Source: Consultant team modeling.

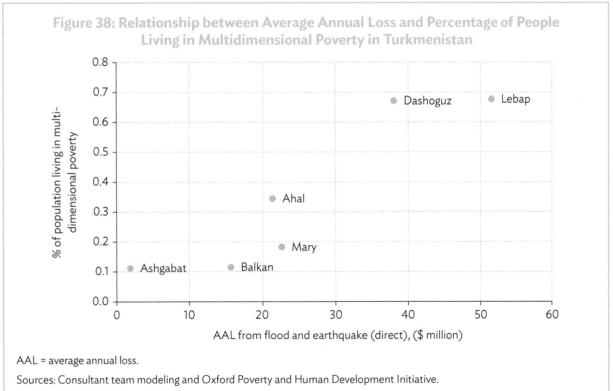

Figure 38: Relationship between Average Annual Loss and Percentage of People Living in Multidimensional Poverty in Turkmenistan

AAL = average annual loss.

Sources: Consultant team modeling and Oxford Poverty and Human Development Initiative.

Risk Retention and Insurance Penetration

In terms of ex ante risk finance instruments, Turkmenistan relies on contingency reserves to support disaster risk response and recovery. These operate at two levels: (i) at the local level, there are local reserve funds which are capped at 2% of relevant budget amounts; and (ii) at the national level, there is a national reserve fund, which has its budget allocated annually. In both cases, resources lapse at the end of each year. However, it has not been possible to identify the resources that might be available in these funds. Beyond these instruments, the government relies on ex post instruments, primarily budget reallocation.

The insurance penetration rate in Turkmenistan, at 0.72% of GDP in 2019, appears relatively high compared to other countries in the region, but this may reflect the monopoly position of the State Insurance Organization of Turkmenistan (Turkmen Gosstrakh). While property insurance against fire and ecological insurance against damage to person or property from pollution are both nominally compulsory, these policies are thought to only cover 1% of dwellings according to a 2009 World Bank review (footnote 122), with market reports suggesting that most insured properties are in and around Ashgabat (footnote 47). Within these policies, earthquake risk is written as an extension to standard property insurance cover with an additional premium charged depending on the zone that the country is in (footnote 47).

Quantifying the Protection Gap

In the absence of information on the amount of resources in the reserve funds in Turkmenistan, it is not possible to provide a quantified assessment of the protection gap comparable to that provided to other countries.

Ability to Rely on Ex Post Borrowing

A lack of official data presents a major challenge in assessing Turkmenistan's debt sustainability and fiscal space, and this limited transparency also makes international borrowing difficult. Turkmenistan received its first recent credit rating from an international credit rating in 2021, with Fitch assigning the country a credit rating of B+, noting that the solid public and external balance sheets were balanced by a low governance ranking, unconventional economic policies, a challenging business environment and some data deficiencies.[128] According to IMF estimates, government debt remains sustainable but has grown significantly over the past 5 years. Revenue mobilization is weak, with tax revenue estimated at 12.9% of GDP in 2019, although the government has broadly run a balanced budget since 2018.[129] The credit rating agency report referred to above notes that, at present, government borrowing needs are met domestically. The limited information that is available is summarized in Figure 39.

Financial inclusion of households has significantly increased since 2011, as measured by bank account ownership. In 2011, only 0.4% of the population had a bank account, compared to 40.6% in 2017. Financial inclusion remains broadly stable across socioeconomic groups, with the poorest 40% of the population having equal rates of account ownership. In 2017, Turkmenistan was the third-best performer in Central Asia in terms of bank account ownership by population.

---

[128] Moody's Investor Service. 2010. *Rating Action: Moody's Withdraws Turkmenistan's Sovereign Ratings.* 9 September. https://www.moodys.com/research/Moodys-Withdraws-Turkmenistans-Sovereign-Ratings--PR_205258.

[129] IMF. 2019. IMF Staff Concludes Staff Visit to Turkmenistan. Press Release No. 19/414. 14 November. https://www.imf.org/en/News/Articles/2019/11/14/pr19414-turkmenistan-imf-staff-concludes-staff-visit.

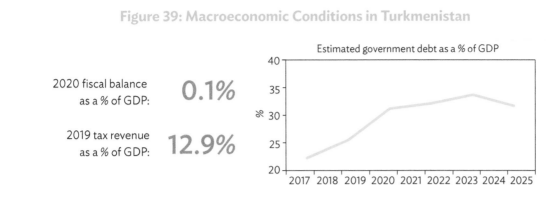

Figure 39: Macroeconomic Conditions in Turkmenistan

2020 fiscal balance as a % of GDP: **0.1%**

2019 tax revenue as a % of GDP: **12.9%**

Estimated government debt as a % of GDP

GDP = gross domestic product.

Note: As the country has only received a credit rating from one credit rating agency, Trading Economics does not provide a synthetic credit rating as it does for other countries. However, a B+ credit rating from Fitch is stated as being equivalent to a rating of 35, which would place the country between the Kyrgyz Republic and Uzbekistan.

Sources: World Bank Open Data https://data.worldbank.org/, and IMF World Economic Outlook Database https://www.imf.org/en/Data (accessed May 2021).

Access to social protection will also help vulnerable groups in responding to disaster events. The social protection available in Turkmenistan includes maternity leave and universal child benefits, along with allowances and homecare services for vulnerable groups, although data on coverage is not available.[130] There are also ongoing efforts to make social protection more shock responsive. The government's Socio-Economic Response Plan, developed in response to the COVID-19 pandemic in partnership with the United Nations country team, calls for a strengthened social protection system by 2021 that will rapidly assess household vulnerability as well as readiness to respond to falling household income.[131]

Summary

The absence of comprehensive, reliable data makes it difficult to provide an overall assessment of the protection gap in Turkmenistan. While reserve funds are in place, the size of these funds, relative to the risks that the country faces, has not been possible to assess. It has also not been possible to assess the extent to which the country can rely on ex post borrowing. Insurance coverage appears low although there have been marked improvements in financial inclusion in recent years.

[130]   United Nations. 2020. *Immediate Socio-Economic Response to Acute Infectious Disease Pandemic in Turkmenistan.* https://reliefweb.int/sites/reliefweb.int/files/resources/TKM_Socioeconomic-Response-Plan_2020.pdf.

[131]   Government of Turkmenistan. 2020. *Immediate Socio-Economic Response Plan to Acute Infectious Disease Pandemic.* https://unsdg.un.org/sites/default/files/2020-08/TKM_Socioeconomic-Response-Plan_2020.pdf.

Uzbekistan

Flood and Earthquake Risk

Both floods and earthquakes are responsible for significant economic losses in Uzbekistan. The AAL associated with floods is $396 million (rising to $415 million when indirect losses are included) while for earthquakes the equivalent figures are $214 million and $238 million. The combined annual average direct losses are equivalent to 0.24% of GNI, which is the third highest of any country in the CAREC region. As Figure 40 shows, high frequency flood events are responsible for greater losses than high frequency earthquakes, but earthquake events with a return period less frequent than 1 in 130 years cause greater losses than flood events of the same return period.

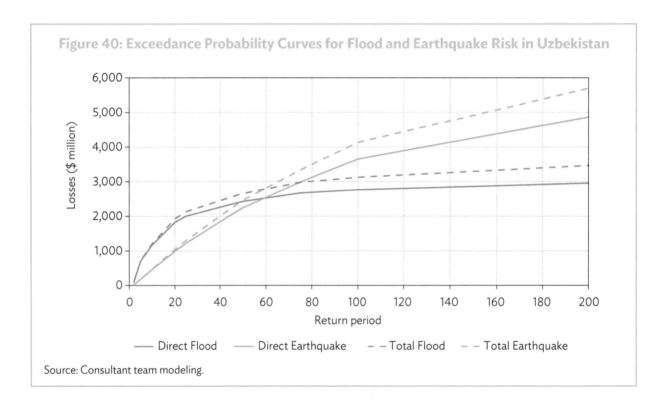

Figure 40: Exceedance Probability Curves for Flood and Earthquake Risk in Uzbekistan

Source: Consultant team modeling.

Correspondingly, these perils are also responsible for significant human losses. Floods are expected to result in an AAL of life of 219 people and earthquakes, a further 92 people. For both perils, this is the third highest across all CAREC countries. The country occupies the same ranking when considering the average number of people severely affected by flood or earthquake with more than 78,000 people expected to be severely affected by floods and almost 22,000 peope severely affected by earthquakes, in an average year.

There is no strong overall correlation between the extent of risk and development outcomes in the country. Nonetheless, as Figure 41 shows, it is striking that the two provinces of the country where AALs are greatest—Andijan and Namangan, both in the east of the country—are also the provinces with some of the lowest HDI scores in the country. These two provinces are also the ones where loss of life from earthquake and floods are expected to be greatest. In both provinces, earthquake and flood risk are responsible for similar levels of AAL. In these two provinces, measured by number of firms, economic activity is concentrated in industrial manufacturing and trade,[132] and these are also the sectors which at a national level account for the largest number of SMEs.[133] However, the statistics from which this analysis is drawn does not account for the important role of *dehkan* farms,[134] which account for around 80% of agricultural production in Uzbekistan. Key agricultural activities in both regions include cotton, cereals, and horticulture.

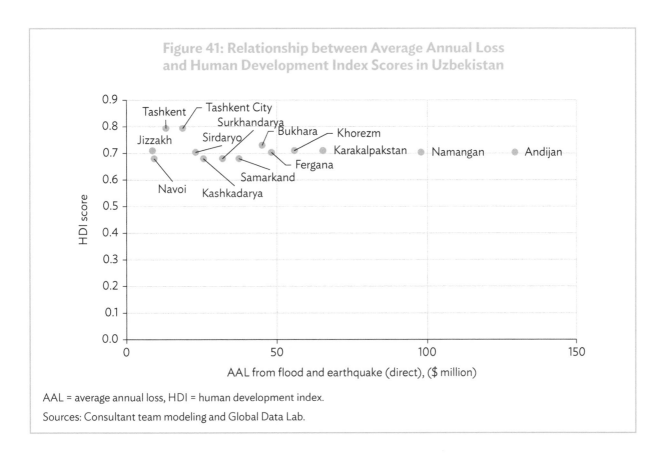

Figure 41: Relationship between Average Annual Loss
and Human Development Index Scores in Uzbekistan

AAL = average annual loss, HDI = human development index.

Sources: Consultant team modeling and Global Data Lab.

Risk Retention and Insurance Penetration

According to the 2019 Resolution of the Cabinet of Ministers,[135] there are three types of financial and material reserves collated by publicly funded bodies:

(i)   Departmental reserves – all national government departments are expected to create financial and material reserves for disaster response and first recovery. These funds are expected to be used in cases of disaster events affecting more than 500 people.

---

[132]   Uzstat. 2021 *Information on Demography of Enterprises and Organizations in the Republic of Uzbekistan.* https://www.stat.uz/images/uploads/reliz2021/registr_may_en.pdf.

[133]   D. Tadjibaeva. 2019. Small and medium sized enterprise finance in Uzbekistan: Challenges and Opportunities. *ADBI Working Paper Series* No. 997. Tokyo: ADBI. https://www.econstor.eu/bitstream/10419/222764/1/1676941622.pdf.

[134]   *Dehkan* farms are family small-scale farming enterprises engaged in the production and sale of agricultural products based on the personal labor of family members on the household plot granted to the head of the family for lifetime lease.

[135]   Resolution of the Cabinet of Ministers of the Republic of Uzbekistan No. 137. 2019. *On Approval of the Regulations on the Procedure for Creating, Using and Restoring Reserves of Financial and Material Resources for Emergency Response.* https://lex.uz/docs/4203375.

(ii) Local reserves – all local government units are expected to create reserves, typically in the form of reserve funds to allow response to disaster events affecting 100–500 people. In 2018, these amounted to around $32 million, ranging from $1 million in Sirdaryo region to $2.9 million in Tashkent City. On average, this amounts to around 1% of the relevant annual budgets for each local government unit.[136]

(iii) Organizational reserves – reserves of organizations funded by the Republic of Uzbekistan, intended to be used for small disaster events affecting no more than 100 people.

In addition, each year the budget allocates funds to the "reserve funds of the Cabinet of Ministers" based on the macroeconomic conditions in the country and the state of the budget. This is a non-accruing fund, and the resources can be used for "timely and flawless financing of unexpected expenditure related to economic, social, cultural and other areas." Under Chapter 5 of the 2019 Resolution, ministries, departments, and local government units can apply for funds allocated to the reserve fund of the Cabinet of Ministers. In 2018, the reserve fund was $32 million (footnote 135).

Finally, the National Road Fund has a dedicated reserve fund for the reconstruction of roads after disaster events. In 2018, the total spending of the Fund was $490 million of which $15 million (3%) was reserved for the response to disaster events (footnote 135).

In total, it is estimated that around $79 million is available for response to disaster events, although most of this funding is not earmarked for disaster events and some of the funding can only be used in relation to road reconstruction. Beyond this, the government would need to make use of budget reallocation, borrowing or external donor funding.

An assessment of disaster risk financing arrangements in Uzbekistan conducted in 2018–2019 (footnote 135) noted that there was no comprehensive post-disaster financing strategy in the country. Some of the issues identified by this review, such as clarity on how the source of financing might vary according to the severity of the disaster event, have now been clarified by the 2019 Resolution. However, other challenges, such as what happens if the reserve fund of the Cabinet of Ministers is exhausted, the aggregation and utilization of disaster impact data to support financial planning and the fact that fiscal risks caused by disaster events seem to be largely unaccounted for by the Government of Uzbekistan appear to remain relevant.

Nonlife insurance penetration rates in Uzbekistan, at 0.3% in 2019, are low compared to other countries in the region (footnote 30). This is despite insurance of mortgaged properties, including against disaster events, being compulsory. As of 2019, approximately 10% of residential dwellings were insured against disaster events,[137] with earthquake cover included as part of the main policy coverage and flood protection provided as a standard extension (footnote 47). The low rates that persist despite these requirements reflect the limited insurance culture. Moreover, commentators have expressed concern that where there is demand, the majority of buyers simply choose the insurance carrier based on the price of coverage, leading to insurance providers to compete on price at the expense of credit quality, capital base, or reinsurance protection (footnote 122).

---

[136]   World Bank. 2018. *Disaster Risk Finance Country Note: Uzbekistan.* http://documents1.worldbank.org/curated/en/513951591597853635/pdf/Disaster-Risk-Finance-Country-Note-Uzbekistan.pdf.

[137]   World Bank. 2020. *Disaster Property Insurance in Uzbekistan: Overview and Recommendations.* https://documents1.worldbank.org/curated/en/617231591599422910/pdf/Disaster-Property-Insurance-in-Uzbekistan-Overview-and-Recommendations.pdf.

Property insurance protection is heavily concentrated in Tashkent City. As of 2012, it was estimated that 60% of collected insurance premiums, across all policy types, derive from the capital.[138] In addition, Uzbekistan does have a relatively large agricultural insurance market that covered 35% of farmers in 2015. The first state-owned agricultural insurer was established in 1997 and enjoyed generous government subsidies. Subsidies were withdrawn in 2002 but the market continued to grow with other firms entering the market.[139] Agricultural losses due to flooding are covered as part of the policy (footnote 47).

Quantifying the Protection Gap

Drawing on the modeling analysis, the protection gap quantification assumes that the AAL from earthquake and flood risk combined is approximately $610 million. In terms of insured losses, given that 10% of residential buildings are covered by property insurance which has earthquake cover as standard, it might be reasonable to assume that 12% of all the losses associated with earthquakes might be covered, taking into account the greater likelihood that nonresidential property assets might be insured. Further, taking account of the data point that approximately 60% of all premiums are paid from policyholders in Tashkent, and the different exposures inside and outside of Tashkent, implied that 45% of the losses from earthquake in Tashkent are insured, and 6% of the losses outside of Tashkent are insured. Flood coverage is then assumed to result in 4.5% and 0.6% of the flood losses inside and outside of Tashkent being insured (i.e., 10% of the proportion of earthquake losses that are insured), reflecting that flood coverage is an optional extra.

Finally, the analysis accounts for $79 million of risk retention being available, although this might be a high-end estimate as some of this funding is intended to be used only for road reconstruction.

The net result of these assumptions is that a significant proportion, around 84%, of the AAL is not covered by existing disaster risk financing instruments. Correspondingly, relatively frequent events are sufficient to exhaust the resources associated with the current disaster risk finance instruments. If the instruments are intended to cover all the losses associated with disaster events, then a 1 in 2-year flood and a 1 in 10-year earthquake would be sufficient to deplete the current provision (regardless of whether indirect losses might also need to be covered by these instruments). If the instruments are intended to only cover emergency responses costs, then they would be depleted by a 1 in 5-year flood event or a 1 in 20-year earthquake event. Figure 42 and Table 12 summarize.

[138] ADB. 2012. *Republic of Uzbekistan: Insurance Sector Development.* https://www.adb.org/sites/default/files/project-document/75049/46112-001-uzb-tar.pdf.

[139] N. Muradullayev, Z. Smailov, and I. Bobjonov. 2016. *Can Insurance Help to Cope with Risks Under Climate Change in Agriculture? An Empirical Evidence from Central Asia?* https://www.iamo.de/fileadmin/user_upload/Bilder_und_Dokumente/06-veranstaltungen/silk_road_2016/presentations_silk_road/2_Muradullaev-Can_insurance_help_to_cope_with_risks_under_climate_change-175_a.pdf.

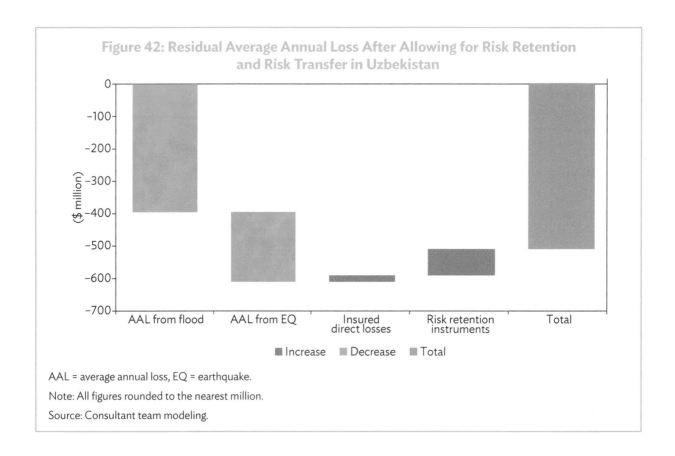

Figure 42: Residual Average Annual Loss After Allowing for Risk Retention and Risk Transfer in Uzbekistan

AAL = average annual loss, EQ = earthquake.

Note: All figures rounded to the nearest million.

Source: Consultant team modeling.

Table 12: Event Frequency at which Ex Ante Mechanisms Are Exhausted in Uzbekistan

Event frequency where direct and indirect losses, less (assumed) insured losses, exceed existing ex ante risk retention		Event frequency where direct losses, less (assumed) insured losses, exceed existing ex ante risk retention		Event frequency where estimated emergency response costs exceed current risk retention mechanisms	
Flood	**Earthquake**	**Flood**	**Earthquake**	**Flood**	**Earthquake**
1 in 2	1 in 10	1 in 2	1 in 10	1 in 5	1 in 20

Source: Consultant team modeling.

Ability to Rely on Ex Post Borrowing

Until the end 2019, Uzbekistan's underlying fiscal position was increasingly robust, although this may now be threatened by the economic fallout from the COVID-19 crisis. Citing low levels of debt and prudent fiscal policy, in May 2020, the IMF considered Uzbekistan's risk of debt distress as "low" and its debt-carrying capacity as "strong."[140] However, the continued fallout from the crisis means that remittances and exports are falling, with the current account deficit expected to widen to 6.4% of GDP in 2021. The fiscal balance is also expected to move into deficit, at 4% of GDP. To retain a sustainable debt position, the country has committed over the medium term to reduce the fiscal deficit to 2% of GDP and has a policy of capping the amount of public debt. This could reduce the country's flexibility to take on debt to help respond to disasters. Figure 43 summarizes data on the macroeconomic conditions in Uzbekistan.

---

[140]   IMF. 2020. *Republic of Uzbekistan – Request for Disbursement Under the Rapid Credit Facility and Purchase Under the Rapid Financing Instrument.* https://www.imf.org/~/media/Files/Publications/CR/2020/English/1UZBEA2020002.ashx.

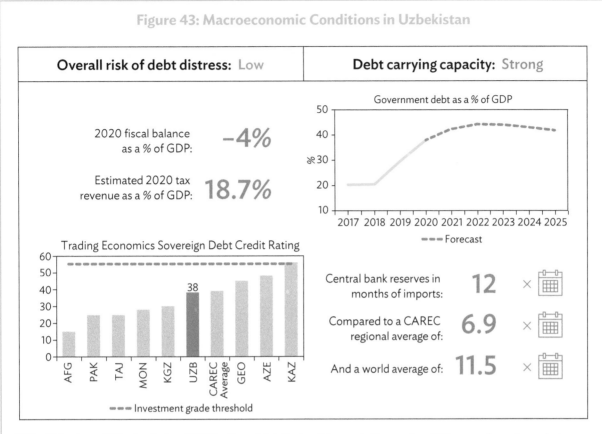

Figure 43: Macroeconomic Conditions in Uzbekistan

AFG = Afghanistan, AZE = Azerbaijan, CAREC = Central Asia Regional Economic Cooperation, GDP = gross domestic product, GEO = Georgia, KAZ = Kazakhstan, KGZ = Kyrgyz Republic, MON = Mongolia, PAK = Pakistan, TAJ = Tajikistan, UZB = Uzbekistan.

Sources: World Bank Open Data https://data.worldbank.org/, IMF World Economic Outlook Database https://www.imf.org/en/ Data, and Trading Economics https://tradingeconomics.com/ (accessed May 2021).

The difficulty in accessing borrowing other than from international institutions is reflected in its approach to the COVID-19 crisis. As of May 2021, international assistance from International Financial Institutions amounted to more than $1.4 billion. This is greater the value of the explicit COVID-19 response measures that had been put in place (footnote 71). More generally, credit rating reports identify that 94% of the overall debt of the country comes from multilateral and bilateral institutions.[141]

Challenges with financial inclusion and the current structure of social protection also mean that households may have difficulty in accessing resources in response to disaster events. Financial inclusion, as measured by bank account ownership, is the fourth lowest in the CAREC region, and fell from 41% to 37% between 2014 and 2017 (footnote 24). The majority of households and firms prefer to use informal methods of finance, such as borrowing from friends and family, and only a few use digital finance, despite reasonable rates of mobile phone ownership.[142]

Spending on social assistance programming, at 0.79% of GDP, is one of the lowest in the CAREC region. Moreover, much of the budget is focused on pensions and child benefits, meaning that unemployment and disability allowance are limited in their coverage and effectiveness in alleviating poverty. Only 30% of the poorest income quintile received any benefit in 2018 (footnote 64).

[141] Fitch Ratings. 2020. *Fitch Affirms Uzbekistan at 'BB-'; Outlook Stable.* https://www.fitchratings.com/research/sovereigns/fitch-affirms-uzbekistan-at-bb-outlook-stable-10-04-2020.
[142] ADB. 2018. *Financial Inclusion, Regulation, and Literacy in Uzbekistan.* https://www.adb.org/publications/financial-inclusion-regulation-literacy-uzbekistan.

Summary

There are important opportunities to improve the disaster risk financing arrangements in Uzbekistan. Insurance penetration is low while existing risk retention mechanisms are only sufficient to cover 1 in 2-year (flood) or 1 in 10-year (earthquake) events if the intention is to cover all losses, or 1 in 5-year (flood) or 1 in 20-year (earthquake) events if the intention is to cover emergency response costs. This points to an obvious coverage gap for more severe events, the typical role for risk transfer instruments. While Uzbekistan's ability to access debt markets as an alternative to risk transfer instruments is more credible than for some other countries in the CAREC region, the source of this borrowing is almost exclusively from international finance institutions. The country retains a sub-investment grade credit rating.

At the same time, there appear to be important opportunities to boost financial inclusion and the design of social protection measures to enhance the financial resilience of the vulnerable sections of the Uzbekistani population. This may be particularly urgent in Andijan and Namangan, which combine significant earthquake and flood risk with relatively low HDI scores.

Alternative Insurance Assumptions

The quantification of the protection gap in the preceding sections relied on assumptions regarding the extent to which losses caused by earthquakes and floods might be insured. While the analysis sought to make assumptions based on evidence, in many cases there is limited detailed data on the penetration of insurance or the extent to which any insurance covers losses. Therefore, this analysis presents two alternative scenarios regarding the proportion of insured losses: one where the proportion of insured losses is twice as high as in the base-case analysis used in section 3 and one where the proportion of insured losses is half that assumed in the base-case analysis.

The results of this analysis are presented in Table A1 and Table A2. These tables show the return period of flood and earthquake event that would cause current risk retention mechanisms to be exhausted, taking account of these alternative insurance assumptions. It considers both the case where risk retention mechanisms are expected to cover both direct and indirect losses, and a case where they are only expected to cover direct losses.[1] The tables illustrate in red those cases where the altered insurance assumption leads to a change in the return period event that causes risk retention mechanisms to be exhausted.

Results show that the analysis under the base case assumptions remains broadly unchanged even when the percentage of losses caused by flood and earthquakes that might be insured increases. Of the 36 data points—nine CAREC countries for which quantification is possible across four different calculations—there are four instances when the sensitivity analysis leads to a change in result compared with the base-case analysis. These cases are:

(i) In Azerbaijan, risk retention mechanisms are only exhausted by the direct and indirect losses caused by a 1 in 50-year flood event rather than a 1 in 25-year flood event and a 1 in 25-year earthquake rather than a 1 in 20-year earthquake. The direct losses are exhausted by a 1 in 50-year earthquake event rather than a 1 in 25-year event;

(ii) In Kazakhstan, risk retention would be sufficient to cover the uninsured direct losses and indirect losses of a 1 in 100-year earthquake event rather than a 1 in 75-year event in the base case.

In none of these cases would these results suggest that the countries in question should be placed in a different category to that proposed in the main report.

Assuming the proportion of insured losses is half that assumed in the central case leads to no changes compared to the base-case analysis (Table A2).

---

[1]   Insurance penetration is not considered when the role of risk retention in covering emergency response costs is analyzed.

Table A1: Event Frequency at which Ex Ante Mechanisms Are Exhausted When Insurance Penetration Is Double That Assumed in the Central Case Analysis

	Event frequency where direct and indirect losses, less (assumed) insured losses, exceed existing ex ante risk retention		Event frequency where direct losses, less (assumed) insured losses, exceed existing ex ante risk retention	
	Flood	Earthquake	Flood	Earthquake
Afghanistan	All	All	All	All
Azerbaijan	1 in 50	1 in 25	1 in 50	1 in 50
Georgia	1 in 5	1 in 20	1 in 5	1 in 25
Kazakhstan	1 in 10	1 in 100	1 in 10	1 in 100
Kyrgyz Republic	1 in 5	1 in 10	In in 5	1 in 10
Mongolia	1 in 10	>1 in 200	1 in 10	>1 in 200
Pakistan	All	All	All	All
PRC, IMAR	NA	NA	NA	NA
PRC, XUAR	NA	NA	NA	NA
Tajikistan	1 in 5	1 in 5	1 in 5	1 in 5
Turkmenistan	NA	NA	NA	NA
Uzbekistan	1 in 2	1 in 10	1 in 2	1 in 10

IMAR = Inner Mongolia Autonomous Region, NA = not available, PRC = People's Republic of China, XUAR = Xinjiang Uygur Autonomous Region.

Source: Consultant team modeling.

Table A2: Event Frequency at which Ex Ante Mechanisms Are Exhausted When Insurance Penetration Is Half That Assumed in the Central Case Analysis

	Event frequency where direct and indirect losses, less (assumed) insured losses, exceed existing ex ante risk retention		Event frequency where direct losses, less (assumed) insured losses, exceed existing ex ante risk retention	
	Flood	Earthquake	Flood	Earthquake
Afghanistan	All	All	All	All
Azerbaijan	1 in 25	1 in 20	1 in 50	1 in 25
Georgia	1 in 5	1 in 20	1 in 5	1 in 25
Kazakhstan	1 in 10	1 in 75	1 in 10	1 in 100
Kyrgyz Republic	1 in 5	1 in 10	1 in 5	1 in 10
Mongolia	1 in 10	>1 in 200	1 in 10	>1 in 200
Pakistan	All	All	All	All
PRC, IMAR	NA	NA	NA	NA
PRC, XUAR	NA	NA	NA	NA
Tajikistan	1 in 5	1 in 5	1 in 5	1 in 5
Turkmenistan	NA	NA	NA	NA
Uzbekistan	1 in 2	1 in 10	1 in 2	1 in 10

IMAR = Inner Mongolia Autonomous Region, NA = not available, PRC = People's Republic of China, XUAR = Xinjiang Uygur Autonomous Region.

Source: Consultant team modeling.

CPSIA information can be obtained
at www.ICGtesting.com
Printed in the USA
BVHW011550021222
653299BV00028B/337